AF600147

THE CATHOLIC UNIVERSITY OF AMERICA
CANON LAW STUDIES
No. 194

The Impediment of Abduction

AN HISTORICAL SYNOPSIS AND COMMENTARY

BY

REV. BARTHOLOMEW FRANCIS L. FAIR,
A.B., S.T.L., J.C.L.
Priest of the Archdiocese of Philadelphia

A DISSERTATION

Submitted to the Faculty of the School of Canon Law of the Catholic University of America in Partial Fulfillment of the Requirements for the Degree of Doctor of Canon Law

THE CATHOLIC UNIVERSITY OF AMERICA PRESS
WASHINGTON, D. C.
1944

Nihil Obstat:

CLEMENS V. BASTNAGEL, J.U.D.,
Censor deputatus.

Washingtonii, D. C., die 6 maii 1944.

Imprimatur:

✠ D. CARD. DOUGHERTY,
Archiepiscopus Philadelphiensis.

Philadelphiae, die 8 maii 1944.

The Walther Printing House
Philadelphia, Pennsylvania

VIRGINI DEIPARAE
ALMAE MATRI NOSTRAE
A FIDUCIA

TABLE OF CONTENTS

INTRODUCTION

The impediment of abduction is one of the safeguards which the Church has established to protect the dignity of the sacrament of matrimony. By assuring to the woman that freedom which is necessary for the proper contracting of so great a sacrament, this impediment preserves inviolate the respect which the dignity of the sacrament requires, since by forced marriages the sacrament would eventually come into disrepute and would be rendered distasteful. This impediment is consequently a fit subject of study, even in the present times, because it shows the interest which the Church maintains in protecting the personal freedom of the individual against encroachment by others.

The present dissertation is a canonical study. It is not primarily historical in its purposes. The summary here given of the history of the impediment is intended to serve the interests of the canonical commentary which follows. It can pretend neither to originality nor to completeness. An attempt has been made to show the general lines of the development of the law of the Church in regard to this impediment and to indicate the principal points which are still open to dispute. The history of the impediment of *raptus* has been a celebrated subject of controversy for many centuries. It is entirely beyond the purposes of this dissertation even to suggest a solution of these historical problems. Rather the problems themselves are only summarily indicated with a view principally to showing the points of contact between these historical questions and the present day law of the Church.

The canonical commentary tries to present a systematic exposition of the present law of the Church on the impediment of abduction. This law has been the product of a long historical evolution; it still enshrines some elements which have been unchanged since the very earliest period of Church history. The interpretation of the text of the modern law cannot therefore abstract from the traditional understanding of the impediment.

In particular the law of the Code of Canon Law depends on the Tridentine legislation, of which it is almost a verbatim repetition. It is for this reason that the present study has been based principally on the classical commentators of the law of the Council of Trent. The numerous commentaries of the Code of Canon Law have also been utilized.

It is a pleasant duty to give expression to the heartfelt gratitude which the writer feels towards His Eminence, the Most Reverend Cardinal Archbishop of Philadelphia, for the opportunity of pursuing advanced studies; towards the Faculty of the School of Canon Law for their unfailing assistance; towards his very many friends — and in particular towards Reverend John L. Nugent of Cornwells Heights, Pa. — for their encouragement and interest which have made happy and enjoyable these past years of study and research.

PRELIMINARY NOTIONS

While the full explanation of the definition of *raptus* must be treated at length in the course of this dissertation, it will be useful to prefix a brief outline of the general meaning of the term and of its principal divisions. Etymologically the word *raptus* means a forcible carrying off. It includes the two ideas of removal from one place to another, and of violence or rapidity in this change of place.[1] While this meaning is occasionally found in its fullest extension even in later usage, generally the term *raptus* is restricted to the violent abduction of persons and the word *rapina* is used in reference to things. *Raptus* may therefore be defined as any violent carrying off of a person from one place to another. In this generic sense the word is used in canon 2354 of the present Code of Canon Law.

Traditionally, however, the word has been understood as referring only to those abductions which were accomplished for sexual gratification, either through marriage or in some illicit fashion. Accepted in this restricted sense *raptus* has been, in Canon Law, both a crime and an impediment, at least since the Council of Trent. It remains such also in the present law of the Church.

There is a distinction, however, between the impediment of *raptus* and the crime. The crime is present whenever a woman is abducted for the purpose of sexual gratification, while the impediment occurs only if the abductor has the intention of taking the woman away in order to marry her. Hence the impediment of *raptus* may be defined as the forcible carrying off of a woman for the purpose of contracting marriage with her.

Two species of such *raptus* are recognized. *Raptus violentiae* is present when a woman is abducted by the use of true force, whether it be physical or moral. *Raptus seductionis* is verified

1 "Aliud esse autem rapi, aliud amoveri palam est, si quidem amoveri etiam sine vi possit, rapi autem sine vi non potest." — D (47, 9) 3, 5.

when a woman, who was at first unwilling, is brought to consent by means of importunate entreaties, promises, flattery, etc. It is closely connected and frequently confused with *raptus in parentes,* which consists in the abduction of a woman who is not yet of age against the will or without the knowledge of her parents or guardians. In *raptus in parentes* there is no violence except that which is committed against the parents.

The extent of the impediment of *raptus* has been greatly increased by the inclusion of a second form of the impediment which is less properly called *raptus.* It consists in the violent detention of a woman either in her own home or in some place to which she has freely come. The Code of Canon Law has included this case under the impediment of *raptus* because of the similarity which the case presents with the condition of a woman who has been abducted.[2]

Although violent retention is not properly the same as abduction, it is convenient to refer to both under the one heading of the impediment of abduction. In the course of this dissertation violent retention and violent abduction will be treated together so far as the subject matter permits. The impediment of abduction may consequently be defined as the violent abduction or detention of a woman for the purpose of contracting marriage with her.

2 C. 1074, §3.

PART ONE

HISTORICAL OUTLINE

CHAPTER I

THE HISTORY OF *RAPTUS* BEFORE THE DECREE OF GRATIAN

Raptus, since it is not only a marriage impediment but also an offense against the public order, was never exclusively a matter for ecclesiastical legislation. The civil authority has constantly proceeded against those guilty of this crime with severe penalties. In fact, before the Church found it necessary to apply its penalties to abductors, the crime had already been for a long time the subject of civil legislation. And when the Church did begin to legislate, she naturally accepted much of this prior legislation of the civil authority as a basis for her own laws. This is especially true of the Roman legislation, for it was from this that the Church adopted the fundamental concept of *raptus*, which became a crime in her law.

The earliest laws, both civil and ecclesiastical, did not consider the relation of *raptus* to marriage directly, but were primarily penal in character, interested in the suppression of the offense against the public order which resulted from *raptus*. Thus the Roman law at first considered it merely as a species of public violence,[1] but soon recognized the specific nature of this crime as connected with sexual gratification.[2]

1 A reflection of this is seen in D (48, 6) where *raptus* is treated under the *Lex Iulia de vi publica.*

2 Cf. München, "Ueber Entführung (raptus) überhaupt und insbesondere als Ehehinderniss." — *Zeitschrift für Philosophie und katholische Theologie* (Köln, 1832-1839; neue Folge, 1840-1852), N. F. II (1841), n. 1, p. 69. (The symbol *ZPkT* will be used hereafter for designating this periodical.)

The idea of *raptus* as a special crime with a distinct and determined concept is found for the first time in a constitution of Constantine the Great in 320.[3] There *raptus* is described as the carrying off of a marriageable person for the purpose of marriage or for some immoral intent. There is no *raptus* if the abduction is perpetrated merely for revenge or for extortion. Some sort of violence must have been committed in the abduction, but this may be directed either against the girl or against her parents. The law itself regards only the case of a woman who was under the *patriapotestas*, but probably the abduction of a woman who had been released from that power was also punished in the same way. It is noteworthy that the only violence necessary in the case of a woman under the *patriapotestas* is that the woman be abducted without the consent of her parents or guardians. Indeed, in this case an essential element of the delict seems to be found in this violation of the right of the parents.[4] If the woman was *sui iuris* the violence had to be directed against her personally.

This Roman law idea of abduction was received into the law of the Church as well. The ecclesiastical texts on *raptus* which date from this period are very few, but the Constantinian notion is apparent in the writings of Saint Basil (+ 379),[5] and is affirmed explicitly a century later in a letter of Pope Saint Gelasius (492-496).[6]

According to Scherer (+ 1918) the ancient Church law included seduction under *raptus*, since it did not distinguish the

3 C Th (9, 24) 1.

4 Cf. Mommsen, *Le droit pénal romain* (tr. par J. Duquesne, 3 vols., Paris, 1907), II, 430.

5 *Epistola canonica ad Amphilochium secunda*, can. 30 — Migne, *Patrologiae cursus completus, series graeca* (161 vols., Parisiis, 1856-1866), XXXII, 724. (The symbol *PG* will hereafter be used in citing this work.)

6 C. 2, C. XXXVI, q. 1. The passage in question is taken from a letter to Hostilius, the date of which is unknown — Jaffé, *Regesta Pontificum Romanorum ab condita Ecclesia ad annum post Christum natum 1198* (2. ed., 2 toms., Lipsiae, 1885-1888), n. 692. (This work will hereafter be cited by the author's name, thus: Jaffé, n.)

two.[7] This does not seem likely. The opinion is based on a text which Gratian attributed to Saint Jerome (+ 420),[8] but which actually appears for the first time in an Irish collection of the seventh or eighth century.[9]

The Church law distinguished between the abduction of a woman who had been espoused and that of a woman who was not. The first canon on *raptus,* canon 11 of the Council of Ancyra (314), treated only of the abduction of an espoused woman.[10]

The Council of Chalcedon in 451, however, without making any reference to espousals punished with excommunication the abduction of any woman.[11]

Neither the Roman law nor the canon law of this period acknowledged any impediment of abduction. The death penalty which had been enjoined for this crime in the Constitution of Constantine made such an impediment meaningless. However, the Roman law naturally did not recognize marriages which were contracted in contravention of this law, as a consequence of an escape from the rather severe penalties. That there were many such marriages is indicated by the presence of two supplementary laws in the *Codex Theodosianus.* The first of these attempted to obtain a better observance of the law by a mitigation of the penalties. It was issued by Constance, the son of Constantine, in 348.[12] The second law, promulgated by the Emperors Valentinian, Valens, and Gratian in 374, recognized the existence of a great number of these invalid and illicit marriages, and regularized their status by decreeing a five-year limit within which the crime might be denounced. If the complaint had not been brought against the marriage within that period, it

7 *Handbuch des Kirchenrechtes* (2 vols., Graz-Leipzig, 1886-1898), II, 378.

8 C. 8, C. XXXVI, q. 2.

9 Cf. Köstler, *Die väterliche Ehebewilligung,* Kirchenrechtliche Abhandlungen, 51 Heft (Stuttgart, 1908), p. 78.

10 C. 45, C. XXVII, q. 2 — Mansi, *Sacrorum conciliorum nova et amplissima collectio* (53 vol. in 59, Paris-Leipzig-Arnheim, 1901-1927), II, 518. (This collection will hereafter be cited simply by the author's name.)

11 C. 1, C. XXXVI, q. 2 — Mansi, VII, 380.

12 C Th (9, 24) 2.

could no longer be made, and the marriage was to be considered valid and the children legitimate.[13]

The ecclesiastical legislation seems to have been even less concerned with the problem of the subsequent marriage of the abductor and his victim. If the woman was espoused to another man, the canon of the Council of Ancyra already quoted required that she be separated from the abductor and returned to her legitimate spouse. The spouse was not, however, obliged to accept her.[14] If she was not espoused to anyone, it seems that marriage between the two depended on the will of her parents. Their consent rendered the marriage licit and valid.[15] Canon 66 of the so-called Canons of the Apostles (5th century), in fact, not only permitted but enjoined the abductor to keep the abducted woman as his wife.[16]

A diriment impediment of abduction appeared for the first time in the codification of the Roman law by Justinian (483-565). The *Corpus iuris civilis* contains several laws on *raptus,* but by far the most important is the title consecrated to this subject in the *Codex.*[17] There is no discussion in this law of the concept of *raptus,* but the notion which Constantine had given in 320 was obviously retained.[18] The impediment which was established was permanent and rendered marriage impossible between the abductor and his victim, even though the parents of the woman had given their consent. The law spoke in the preamble of *virgines honestae* and the later interpretation concluded from this that the abduction of a woman who was not

13 C Th (9, 24) 3.

14 S. Basil, *Epistola canonica ad Amphilochium secunda,* can. 22 — *PG,* XXXII, 724.

15 Mitterer, *Geschichte des Ehehindernisses der Entführung im kanonischen Recht seit Gratian,* Görres-Gesellschaft zur Pflege der Wissenschaft im katholischen Deutschland. Veröffentlichungen der Sektion für Rechts und Sozialwissenschaft, 43 Heft (Paderborn, 1924), p. 14-15. This work will hereafter be cited thus: Mitterer, *Geschichte.*

16 Mansi, I, 43.

17 C (9, 13).

18 Cf. C (9, 13) 1. The same concept appears in the two *Novellae* which interpret this law (N 143 and 150).

respectable was not punished in the law.[19] This law affected all those who were still in their father's power (i.e., maidens and widows) and also women who had been emancipated from that power, if they were still under twenty-five years of age.[20]

There is much controversy, even in recent times, on the proper interpretation of this law. The principal points of discussion are whether or not the law punished the abduction of one's own betrothed, as the later interpretation certainly maintained,[21] and whether the marriage of a woman without parental consent was here considered *raptus*.[22]

The Church law continued to depend on the Councils of Ancyra and Chalcedon and the Canons of the Apostles. These three laws had been included in the Collection of Dionysius Exiguus (c. 510) and were therefore known in the Western Church The concept of *raptus* remained that of the Roman law, and in particular that of the Roman law as it had been used by Gelasius at the end of the fifth century, i.e., as derived from the Theodosian Code. The punishments of *raptus* were not inflicted on the abductor who carried off his own betrothed. This is explicitly stated by the Roman Councils of 721[23] and 743.[24] It is uncertain in the canon law, too, whether or not the marriage of a woman without her parent's consent constituted a crime of *raptus* in this period.[25]

The Church in Italy does not seem to have legislated at all concerning the validity of the marriage between the abductor and his victim. The Council of Ravenna (877) commanded that the

19 Cf. Mitterer, *Geschichte*, p. 7, note 2.

20 Cf. N (115, 3) 11. Köstler, *Die väterliche Ehebewilligung*, pp. 23-24.

21 There is question here of an interpolation in the text. Cf. München, "Ueber Entführung . . ." in *ZPkT*, N. F., II, n. 2, pp. 68-72; Mitterer, *Geschichte*, p. 8.

22 Cf. Mitterer, *Geschichte*, p. 9.

23 Can. 10-11 — Mansi, XII, 264.

24 Can. 7 — Mansi, XII, 383.

25 This dispute concerns especially the meaning of can. 6 of the Council held at Ravenna in 877 (Mansi, XVII, 383). Cf. Köstler (*Die väterliche Ehebewilligung*, p. 71) who asserts the presence of the crime, and Mitterer (*Geschichte*, pp. 17-18) who denies it.

abducted woman should be separated from the abductor, but nothing is said concerning the possibility of marriage once this separation has taken place.[26] It is not certain whether Nicholas I (858-867), in treating of the abduction of the daughter of Charles the Bald, considered the marriage as valid or not, but, at any rate, the Pope may have had the Frankish Church laws in mind, which were somewhat stricter as regards the subsequent marriage of the parties.[27]

The canon law developed somewhat differently in the Frankish kingdoms. The Roman law concept of *raptus* was the foundation on which the later law developed,[28] but it appears certain that marriage of a woman without her parents' consent was considered *raptus.*[29] Seduction is treated in the canonical texts of this period very frequently together with *raptus* and is assigned the same effects. It was probably also considered a species of *raptus,* particularly since in the case of seduction parental consent was lacking.[30]

The earliest texts that certainly establish an impediment are found in the first half of the ninth century. The capitulary of Aix-la-Chapelle of 817 states in chapter 23 that the abductor could not according to the canonical authority contract legitimate marriage *(coniugia legitima)* with the person he had abducted. In the following chapter there are special norms with reference to the abduction of women who had already been espoused by someone other than the abductor.[31] These laws evidently did not obtain the desired effect, for in 845 the Coun-

26 Can. 6 — Mansi, XVII, 383.

27 Köstler, *Die väterliche Ehebewilligung*, p. 72; Mitterer, *Geschichte*, pp. 16, 17, 19.

28 I Council of Orleans (511), can. 1 — *Monumenta Germaniae historica, Concilia*, tom. I, *Concilia aevi merovingici* (ed. F. Maasen, Hannoverae, 1893), p. 3; cf. Köstler, *op. cit.*, p. 82, note 3.

29 Cf. Köstler, *op. cit.*, pp. 80-102; Mitterer, *Geschichte*, pp. 11-12.

30 Cf. Scherer, *Handbuch des Kirchenrechtes*, II, 378, note 7; Köstler, *op. cit.*, p. 89.

31 *Monumenta Germaniae historica*, Legum Sectio II, *Capitularia Regum Francorum*, tom. I (ed. A. Boretius, Hannoverae, 1883), p. 279; cf. München, "Ueber Entführung . . ." in *ZPkT*, N. F., II, n. 3, pp. 13-15.

cil of Meaux again considered the question of *raptus* and, after establishing various temporary norms to regularize the many marriages which had been contracted through abduction, declared that abductors in the future should be deprived of all hope of marriage.[32] It is not clear in the text whether or not the impediment forbade marriage with persons other than the abducted woman. The impediment is certainly however both diriment and permanent in its effects.

The impediment appears also in the spurious collections of this period, notably in the collection of Benedict the Levite,[33] as well as in the ecclesiastical literature.[34]

These strict prescriptions were evidently not fully observed in practice, for there was a gradual relaxation in the discipline of the Church.[35] This tendency in the practice of the Church can be deduced from the difficulty which was experienced by Gratian in reconciling the legal texts and the ecclesiastical discipline. The final stage in this relaxation of the rigor of the canons was reached in the period following Gratian when the impediment of abduction practically disappeared from the law of the Church.

32 Can. 66 — Mansi, XIV, 834.

33 III, 395 — *Monumenta Germaniae historica, Leges,* tom. II (ed. Pertz, Hannoverae, 1837), p. 127.

34 E.g., Hincmar of Rheims (+ 879), *De coercendo raptu viduarum, puellarum et sanctimonialium* — Migne, *Patrologiae cursus completus, series latina* (221 vols., Parisiis, 1844-1864), CXXV, 1017-1036.

35 Cf., e.g., n. 65 of the Arundel Penitentiary which permitted marriage between the abductor and his victim provided that the woman freely consented. The text is in Schmitz, *Die Bussbücher und die Bussdisciplin der Kirche* (Mainz, 1883), p. 455. The place and time of the composition of this work are not certainly known, but it is most probable that it was of Gallican origin sometime after the year 895. Cf. Liebermann, "Zum Poenitentiale Arundel" — *Zeitschrift der Savigny-Stiftung für Rechtsgeschichte, Kanonistische Abteilung* (Weimar, 1911-), XV (1926), 531-532; Fournier, "Études sur les pénitentiels, V" — *Revue d'histoire et de littérature religeuses* (1896-1907, N.S., 1910-), IX (1904), 98-99; Schmitz, *op. cit.*, 432-436.

CHAPTER II

FROM THE DECREE OF GRATIAN TO THE COUNCIL OF TRENT

Article I — The Teaching of Gratian

The Decree of Gratian reflects the confused state in which canonical teaching and practice found itself in the eleventh century. The canons of the Frankish councils had introduced the impediment, but they had never been received officially in the rest of the Church. The supreme authority of the Church, the Pope, had never constituted such an impediment. At the same time, the Frankish canons had been inserted in some of the canonical collections and so were influential in molding canonical thought. Canonical practice, however, must have followed in general the milder Roman practice. That can easily be deduced from the forced argumentation with which Gratian justified his own less severe conclusion.

Gratian treated of *raptus* in the thirty-sixth Cause of the second part of his *Decretum*, and considered it in direct relation to marriage. The case with which he introduced his discussion is as follows: A certain young man had invited a girl to dine with him and had induced her through gifts to accept his invitation. After the meal, he violated the girl. Her parents, on hearing this, gave her to the young man in marriage. He then provided the dowry,[1] and publicly married her. The Magister proposed two questions: Did the young man in question commit the crime of *raptus*, and could the *raptor* be joined in marriage with the woman against whom he had offended?

In answering the first of these queries Gratian developed his concept of *raptus*. On the basis of a text of St. Isidore

[1] This was one of the civil (Roman) law punishments of *raptus* — C (9, 13).

(+ 636)[2] and the text of Saint Gelasius which was cited above, *raptus* is defined by Gratian as the forcible carrying off of a woman from her father's house with the purpose of defiling her and holding her as a wife. The violence may be directed against the girl alone, against her parents alone, or against both.[3] This is, of course, in substance the Roman law definition of *raptus*. The crime is committed even when there has been no actual violence against the woman abducted, provided that the parents are opposed.[4] It is likewise a case of *raptus* if, while the parents are in accord with the abductor, the girl herself is opposed.

Little if any information is given in the text of Gratian from which to decide what species of violence was necessary. Nevertheless there seems to be agreement among the authors that Gratian recognized both physical violence and moral violence, if this last be understood of threats and the inflicting of grave fear.[5] That the violence need not be committed in the actual abduction but may occur through the forcible violation of the woman is apparent from the text of Gratian itself.[6] Indeed, the crime known in modern English as rape seems to have been *raptus* even independently of any abduction. In this case, however, violence probably had to be used directly against the girl: the

2 C. 1, C. XXXVI, q. 1—*Etymologiae*, V, 26, 14. Cf. Lindsay, *Isidori Hispalensis episcopi etymologiarum sive originum libri*, Scriptorum classicorum bibliotheca Oxoniensis, Oxonii, 1910.

3 "Raptus admittitur cum puella violenter a domo patris abducitur, ut corrupta in uxorem habeatur, sive puellae solummodo, sive parentibus tantum, sive utrisque vis illata constiterit . . ." — *Dictum* p. c. 2, C. XXXVI, q. 1.

4 *Loc. cit.* Köstler's opinion (*Die väterliche Ehebewilligunng*, p. 109) that the crime also existed when the parents merely did not know of the girl's abduction seems to be based on insufficient evidence. Cf. Mitterer, *Geschichte*, p. 42, note 2; pp. 43-45.

5 The only text in which Gratian directly treated of this question is the *Dictum* p. c. 3, C. XXXVI, q. 1. There he denied that promises were sufficient to cause violence. Further specification of Gratian's opinion seems to be without foundation in the text. Cf. Plöchl, *Das Eherecht des Magisters Gratianus*, Wiener Staats- und Rechstwissenschaftliche Studien, Band XXIV (Leipzig-Wien: Deuticke, 1935), p. 60.

6 *Dictum* p. c. 3, C. XXXVI, q. 1.

defloration of a girl with her consent but against the will of the parents would not have been considered a crime of *raptus*.[7] It is disputed whether or not carnal intercourse was a necessary element in Gratian's concept of *raptus*.[8]

In one important respect Gratian differed from the Roman law idea of *raptus:* he recognized no possibility of an abduction of one's own betrothed. Under these circumstances abduction was not possible even when it took place against the will of both the woman and her parents, provided, of course, that true legal and valid *sponsalia* had preceded.[9]

Gratian declared the impediment of *raptus* to be present not only in the case of the abduction of a person who was betrothed to someone other than the abductor, but also in the case of the abduction of an unbetrothed person.[10] In the first case, however, there was a diriment and permanent impediment, so that the abductor could not marry the abducted spouse of another under any conditions. In the case of an unbetrothed person, on the contrary, there was a diriment impediment between the two, but it was not permanent. The impediment ceased when certain conditions were fulfilled. These conditions were: the restitution of the girl to her parents, the performance of penance by the guilty party or parties, and the obtaining of the consent of the parents of both parties or at least of the girl.[11] These conditions seem to be required for the very validity of the subsequent marriage, but there is some discussion as to the necessity of some of them. Thus, while Freisen considers that the removal of the impediment depended precisely on the previous necessary performance of penance,[12] Mitterer recognizes no absolute ne-

7 Cf. Mitterer, *Geschichte*, pp. 48-49.

8 Cf. Mitterer, *Geschichte*, p. 46, note 1; Freisen (1932), *Geschichte des canonischen Eherechts* (zweite Ausgabe, Paderborn, 1893), p. 593; Plöchl, *op. cit.*, p. 60, note 8.

9 Cf. Mitterer, *Geschichte*, pp. 29-30; Freisen, *Geschichte des canonischen Eherechts*, pp. 590-593.

10 C. 34, C. XXVII, q. 2; *dictum* p. c. 6, C. XXXVI, q. 2.

11 *Dictum* p. c. 7, C. XXXVI, q. 2; *dictum* p. c. 11, C. XXXVI, q. 2.

12 *Geschichte des canonischen Eherechts*, p. 608. Freisen, in fact, denies

cessity of such previous performance of penance for the lapsing of the impediment.[13] There is general agreement, however, as to the necessity of parental consent in the case of marriage after *raptus,* even though it is certain that parental consent was not required by Gratian for the contracting of valid marriage in ordinary circumstances.[14]

Article II — The Teaching of the Decretists

The teaching of Gratian on *raptus* was given a logical development in the writings of his successors, the Decretists. These commentators of Gratian clarified somewhat his concept of *raptus* and faithfully mirrored the gradual liberalization of the impediment which was taking place in the canonical practice of the time.

Thus, so far as the concept of abduction was concerned, they were at one with Gratian in designating rape as *raptus.*[15] In the question of *raptus* as committed through violence against the parents alone, Rufinus (+ 1190), with the majority of the other commentators, taught that there was no abduction when the woman consented to the abductor, provided that the woman was old enough to become married and that the abduction was intended for marriage and not for some immoral purpose.[16] This was merely a consequence of the canonical teaching relative to the question of the necessity of parental consent for marriage. Although Gratian had taught that parental consent was not absolutely necessary, he had nevertheless failed to draw the full

the existence of any separate impediment of *raptus.* The impediment, he maintains, is really that of public penance.

13 *Geschichte,* pp. 53-56.

14 Cf. Freisen, *op. cit.,* p. 608; Mitterer, *Geschichte,* p. 53; Plöchl, *Das Eherechts des Magisters Gratianus,* pp. 61-62.

15 Cf., e.g., the signed Gloss of Ioannes Teutonicus (+ 1245) — *Gl. Ord.,* c. 34, C. XXVII, q. 2 ad v. "rapuerit"; Bernard of Pavia (+ 1213), *Summa Decretalium* (ed. Laspeyres, Ratisbonae, 1860), V, 14, §1 — p. 231.

16 *Summa Decretorum* (ed. Singer, Paderborn, 1902), C. XXXVI, q. 1, ad v. "Vis infertur puellae et non parentibus" — p. 535. For the other Decretists, cf. Mitterer, *Geschichte,* pp. 57-59.

conclusion from this teaching in his treatment of *raptus*. The Decretists merely inserted here the inference which they had drawn from his teaching in C. XXXII.[17] The Decretists concurred with Gratian in teaching that there could be no question of the crime of *raptus* in the abduction of a woman betrothed to the abductor.

In treating of the effect of abduction or rape on marriage, the Decretists distinguished clearly between the abduction of a woman who was betrothed to someone other than the abductor and the abduction of a woman who had not been betrothed. In the first case they recognized the existence of an impediment, but they were not in agreement as to its character. The difficulty derived from the necessity, acknowledged at that time, of inserting the newly excogitated distinction between the *sponsa de praesenti* and the *sponsa de futuro* into the canonical teaching on *raptus*. There was general agreement, however, that the abduction of another's betrothed caused at least a prohibitive impediment.[18] Huguccio (+ 1210) taught that if it were a *sponsa de praesenti* who was abducted, there was a diriment impediment, but that only a prohibitive impediment existed in the case of a *sponsa de futuro*. He spoke, though, only of the impediment which prevented marriage between the abductor and the woman abducted, and not of the absolute impediment of which Gratian treated in C. XXVII.[19]

In the question of the impediment which existed for a man who had abducted an unbetrothed person, the Glossators of the Decree of Gratian in general accepted his conclusion while rejecting in the main the arguments on which he based it. Marriage was, in their teaching, always permitted between the abductor and his victim as long as the girl consented and there existed no other reason which prohibited the marriage. *Raptus*, however, was to be carefully distinguished. If the crime was committed for an immoral purpose *(raptus ad stuprum)*, then the parties

17 Cf. cc. 12 sqq., C. XXXII, q. 2.

18 Cf. *Gl. Ord.*, c. 11, C. XXXIII, q. 2, ad. v. "Poenitentibus."

19 *Gl.* ad C. XXXVI, q. 2, ad v. "Nunc quaeritur" — cited by Mitterer, *Geschichte*, p. 65, note 3.

were to be separated. Even if the girl consented in these evil intentions, the separation of the parties was still demanded. If nonetheless she consented to marry her abductor, the marriage was valid. If she had been abducted for marriage, on the other hand, then the woman's consent, whether antecedent or subsequent to the abduction, warranted the validity of the marriage. Of course, if the girl was not of an age at which marriage was possible *(puella innubilis)*, then her consent was not sufficient until she had attained the requisite age.[20]

Article III — The Decretal Law

The *Corpus iuris canonici* contains only two decretals which treat of the impediment of abduction. They are both from a very early period in the Decretal law (the end of the twelfth century). They represent the discipline which was in force in the Church until the time of the Council of Trent.

The first and the more important of these decretals is the *Cum Causam* of Lucius III (1181-1185).[21] The text of this law is very obscure and the decretal has therefore been a subject of controversy from very early times.[22] According to one interpretation of the text, this law introduced an important change into the canonical concept of *raptus*. The decretal was, according to this explanation, concerned with a case of *raptus in parentes* and declared that so long as the woman was willing, there was no crime of abduction, at least if the abductor had made some previous overtures concerning marriage.[23]

20 Rufinus, *Summa Decretorum*, C. XXXVI, q. 1, ad v. "Vis infertur puellae et non parentibus" — *ed. cit.*, p. 534; Bernard of Pavia, *Summa de matrimonio*, n. 9 — *ed. cit.*, p. 301.

21 C. 6, X, *de raptoribus*, V, 17 — c. 4, Comp. I, V, 14; Jaffé, II, n. 15184. The exact date within the pontificate of Lucius III and the name of the bishop to whom it was addressed are uncertain.

22 Cf., e.g., Hostiensis (+ 1271), *Commentaria in quintum Decretalium librum* (Venetiis, 1581), c. 6, X, *de raptoribus*, V, 17; Ioannes ab Anania (+ 1457), *Praelectiones in Decretalium librum quintum* (Lugduni, 1546), c. 6, X, *de raptoribus*, V, 17.

23 Cf. Salman, "Interpretation des Caput VI, *Cum Causam*, X, *de rap-*

Other authors, however, understood the decretal as treating of a case in which a man had abducted his own betrothed, and consequently they were of the opinion that no change was introduced into the concept of *raptus*.[24]

With the issuance of the Decretal *Accedens* of Innocent III (1198-1216), the impediment of abduction as a separate and distinct hindrance to marriage practically disappeared from the law. This decretal declared that the abducted woman could lawfully *(legitime)* contract marriage with her abductor provided that her lack of consent had changed into consent, and that the parties were canonically capable of contracting.[25] Abduction, therefore, became a species of the impediment of force and fear.

The commentators on the Decretals continued the traditional teaching on *raptus* with the necessary modifications introduced by the laws of Lucius III and Innocent III. Thus, many of them continued to speak of rape as a species of raptus.[26] But the influence of Roman law on these authors was very strong; hence, there were some borrowings from Roman law introduced into the canon law. For example, many writers of this period stated that the impediment of *raptus* did not arise when a corrupt woman or a prostitute was abducted.[27]

The canonical tradition was followed, nonetheless, on the question of the abduction of one's own betrothed. Here the Roman law recognized a crime of *raptus*, but the canon law

toribus, V, 17"—*Archiv für katholisches Kirchenrecht* (Innsbruck, 1857-1862; Mainz, 1862-) LXVI (1891), 108-122. This periodical will hereafter be cited with the symbol *AKKR*.

24 This interpretation is sustained by Dilloo, "Interpretation des cap. 6, X, *de raptoribus*, V, 17" in *AKKR*, LXXV (1896), 329-336.

25 C. 7, X, *de raptoribus*, V, 17—c. un., Comp. III, V, 9; Potthast, *Regesta Pontificum Romanorum* (2 vols., Berolini, 1874-1875), n. 1066. This decretal dates from May or June of 1200, but it is not certain to whom it was addressed.

26 Cf., e.g., Aegidius Bellamerae (+ 1392), *Commentaria in Gratiani Decreta* (Lugduni, 1550), c. 2, C. XXXVI, q. 1, ad. v. "raptus."

27 E.g., Hostiensis, *Summa aurea* (Venetiis, 1570), lib. V, *de poenis raptorum corporum*, 1. Cf. *supra*, p. 4.

did not.[28] In the question of *raptus in parentes*, the teaching is not clearly defined. Thus the *Glossa Ordinaria* stated absolutely that there was no *raptus* when the girl had consented.[29]

Panormitanus repudiated this latter statement. He asserted that the impediment was present unless there had been some previous approaches by the abductor about the marriage. It seems from the text of Panormitanus that such approaches essentially had to be made to the parents of the girl. In reality, however, the requirement of this circumstance in the approaches appears to have been demanded with a view to obtaining assurance that the woman was abducted for the purpose of marriage, and not for some other reason. Nevertheless, if the parents objected to the man's desire to marry the woman, the man did not commit the crime of *raptus* by abducting the woman. In the opinion of Panormitanus, the impediment of *raptus in parentes* still existed in the law. It was present whenever a minor girl was abducted against the will or without the knowledge of the parents, even though with her own consent, provided that the abductor had not previously contacted the parents in regard to the marriage.[30]

Since the impediment had practically been reduced to a presumption of non-consent on the part of the woman, it was given less attention during this period. The Decretal *Accedens* had specified that marriage was possible so long as the persons concerned were lawfully capable of contracting marriage. Although there has been some discussion in later times concerning the meaning of this expression,[31] the commentators of the period immediately following the decretal understood it as indicating the absence of any canonical impediment, and in particular the absence of the impediment arising from deficient age.[32] The

28 Panormitanus (Nicholaus de Tudeschis, + 1453), *Commentaria in quartum et quintum librum Decretalium* (Venetiis, 1588), c. 6, X, *de raptoribus*, V, 17.

29 *Gl. Ord.*, c. 6, X, *de raptoribus*, V, 17, ad v. "Dicatur admitti."

30 Panormitamus, *Commentaria*, c. 6, X, *de raptoribus*, V. 17.

31 Cf. Mitterer, *Geschichte*, pp. 80-81.

32 Ioannes Andreae (1270-1348), *Novella super quinto Decretalium* (Venitiis, 1504), c. 7, X, *de raptoribus*, V, 17.

teaching that *raptus* induced only a presumption of non-consent was so understood that the consent which was necessary for a valid marriage could be given even tacitly, provided that it was perfectly free and in some way manifested.[33]

During this period there remained a prohibitive impediment which forbade the marriage of an abductor with an espoused woman whom he had abducted. This impediment, however, was probably not an impediment of *raptus,* but rather the impediment which arose from a valid betrothal. Betrothal, in fact, established a prohibitive impediment which forbade marriage for either party with anyone other than the proper betrothed.

33 Ioannes ab Anania, *Praelectiones in Decretalium librum quintum,* c. 7, X, *de raptoribus,* V, 17.

CHAPTER III

FROM THE COUNCIL OF TRENT TO THE CODE OF CANON LAW

Article I — The Council of Trent

The Decretal legislation, while it required a free consent for the validity of a marriage between the abductor and his victim, provided no norms by which the presence of this freedom in the consent could be assured. Thus the marriage of an abducted woman received practically the same treatment as the marriage of any other woman, despite the fact that there was naturally a strong presumption against freedom of consent when the expression of consent was given by an abducted woman who remained under the influence of her abductor. The Council of Trent, in line with its general policy of insuring, so far as it was possible, the freedom of the parties to the marriage contract, remedied this situation by setting a definite set of circumstances in which the consent of an abducted woman had to find its expression if it was to obtain juridic effect. Accordingly it re-established the impediment of abduction: no longer, however, as a permanent impediment, but as a temporary one, which ceased as soon as the parties fulfilled the conditions of the law. The cessation depended entirely on the will of the parties themselves: when the woman had been separated from her abductor and placed in a free and secure place, she could give a valid consent to marriage with the abductor. Until this was done, she could not give a juridically effective consent.

In this way the Council avoided the two extreme measures which had been proposed. On the one hand, the abductor was not forced into marriage with his victim, as the original draft of the legislation had proposed,[1] and, on the other hand, marriage

[1] Cf. *Concilium Tridentinum, Diariorum, Actorum, Epistolarum, Tractatum nova collectio* (edidit Societas Goerresiana, 13 vols. [incomplete], Friburgi Brisgoviae, 1901-), IX, 684.

between the two parties was not made impossible by a permanent impediment, as some of the Fathers of the Council had requested.[2] At the same time the freedom of the woman's consent was protected by the requirement that she be removed entirely from the influence of the abductor before she could give valid expression to a free consent. The Decree of the Council reads as follows:

> Decernit sancta synodus, inter raptorem et raptam, quamdiu in potestate raptoris manserit, nullum posse consistere matrimonium. Quodsi rapta, a raptore separata et in loco tuto et libero constituta, illum in virum habere consenserit, eam raptor in uxorem habeat; et nihilominus raptor ipse, ac omnes illi consilium, auxilium et favorem praebentes, sint ipso jure excommunicati ac perpetuo infames, omniumque dignitatum incapaces. Et si clerici fuerint, de proprio gradu decidant. Teneatur praeterea raptor, mulierem raptam, sive eam in uxorem duxerit sive non duxerit, decenter arbitrio judicis dotare.[3]

While the law was in itself clear, it became the subject of much controversy in the centuries which followed the Council. This was due primarily to the fact that it gave no definition of *raptus*. This concept had to be derived from the preceding legislation, which was itself very confused in regard to this point. Together with this difficulty of determining how much of the old law was preserved in the Council's decree, there was also the problem of applying the law in accord with the known desire of the Council in regard to the protection of the freedom of the parties.

[2] *Op. cit.*, IX, 746.

[3] Conc. Tridentinum, sess. XXIV, *de ref. matrim.*, c. 6. It is uncertain what influences induced the Council to legislate on abduction, although it may have been at the request of the French bishops and royal representatives. The reigning Pontiff, Pius IV, supported the prospective legislation from the very beginning. The French, however, according to Sarpi, were not satisfied with the law as it was finally enacted. Cf. Pallavicino (+ 1677), *Istoria del Concilio di Trento* (6 vols., Faenza, 1792-1797), V, 177, 293; Esmein, *Le mariage en droit canonique* (2. ed. par Génestal et Dauvillier, 2 toms., Paris: Recueil Sirey, 1929-1935), II, 208.

The law on abduction received further development in the period succeeding the Council of Trent mainly through doctrinal interpretation and canonical jurisprudence, rather than from legislative enactment or administrative ordinance. In the case of *raptus in parentes,* the decisions of the Congregation of the Council played a very large part. Nevertheless, the law itself did not change; the legislation of the Council of Trent was still the ruling law when the Code of Canon Law was introduced. The Code itself likewise did not effect any change in the law, but rather, by the addition of a few words, clarified the former law. Most of these clarifications had, as a matter of fact, already become the common canonical interpretation even before the Code.

Since the canonical commentary which follows will deal with the Code law which is materially the same as that of Trent, it would be superfluous to describe here the various points on which the doctrinal interpretation of the post-Tridentine canonists contributed to the better understanding of the law. In the course of the commentary these matters will again require notice. The reader is therefore referred to the canonical commentary for the evolution of canonical thought on the Council of Trent's law. There remains, however, the question of *raptus in parentes,* which was frequently submitted to the judicial authority of the Church. The interpretation of the decisions of the Congregation of the Council and of the Sacred Roman Rota is primarily an historical question, and, though it must needs affect the theoretical interpretation even of the present legislation, is more conveniently set forth in the following article.

Article II — The Impediment in the Case of Raptus in Parentes

Raptus in parentes was present whenever a girl of minor age, notwithstanding her own consent both to the abduction and to the intended marriage, was abducted against the will of her parents or her guardians. In this case, according to the Roman civil law, there was a crime (and consequently a civil impediment) of abduction because of the injury which was done to the rights of the parents or guardians. At least for a time this same view obtained in canon law.[4] Whether or not it continued current during the Decretal period remains a subject of controversy, although the better view seems to be that it was not then considered a crime or an obstacle to marriage.[5]

Since the Council of Trent did not change the extension of the two terms *raptor* and *rapta,* the same doubt as to the existence of the impediment of *raptus in parentes* remained after the Tridentine legislation.

A proposal which would have definitely settled the controvery had been presented to the Council. Cardinal Madruzzo (+ 1578) had suggested that the Council declare marriage impossible between an abductor and his unwilling victim, but possible between an abductor and a girl who was willingly abducted.[6] Several bishops concurred with the Cardinal in this suggestion,[7] but the suggestion was not followed.[8]

It is hardly permissible to argue from this that the Council wished to sanction the stricter view. Had the Cardinal's proposal been adopted, not only would there have been no impediment in the case of *raptus in parentes,* but there also would have been none if the girl had consented to the abduction, even though she had been fraudulently induced to give such a consent. Hence, whatever deduction may be drawn from the rejection of this proposal, it can contribute nothing toward the solution of the problem at hand.

Navarrus (1493-1586), who wrote but a short time after the Council, was of the opinion that *raptus in parentes* did give rise to an impediment.[9] Not long afterwards, however, the

4 Cf. *dictum* p. c. 3, C. XXXVI, q. 1.

5 Cf. Mitterer, *Geschichte,* pp. 80-82.

6 *Concilium Tridentinum,* IX, 695.

7 *Concilium Tridentinum,* IX, 746.

8 *Concilium Tridentinum,* IX, 970.

9 *Consilia seu responsa* (2 vols., Venetiis, 1621), lib. V, tit. *de raptoribus,* cons. II.

contrary view was again proposed by Sanchez (1550-1610). He taught a careful distinction between the case in which the parents were positively opposed to the abduction and that in which they were merely ignorant of it. If they simply were ignorant, then there was no violence against them and hence there would be no *raptus* in the proper sense. Their rights were violated, it is true, and consequently there was a crime, but it was not the crime of *raptus,* which by definition implied a violent carrying off. If they positively dissented then there was a true crime of abduction, but this did not come under the impediment treated by the Council of Trent, because that impediment was intended primarily to protect the liberty of the girl which was not in any way jeopardized in the case proposed.[10]

This distinction was not admitted by the followers of the opposite opinion, and there continued to be some authors who believed the impediment to be present even when the parents were only ignorant of the abduction of their children of minor age.[11]

Cardinal De Luca (1614-1693) adopted the stricter view and explained it further. According to his teaching, the impediment was present whenever a girl of minor age was abducted if her parents or guardians were opposed to or ignorant of the abduction. One exception was to be made: if some negotiations *(tractatus)* had been made by the abductor for the purpose of obtaining the girl in marriage, then there was no impediment if he abducted her. These negotiations, however, had to be the practical equivalent of the full legal *sponsalia,* i.e., an actual betrothal binding both parties.[12] This exception, based on the decretal *Cum Causam,* was widened by other authors, who held

10 *Disputationes de sancto matrimonii sacramento* (3 toms. in 1, Antverpiae, 1626), lib. VII, disp. XII, n. 13, n. 35; disp. XIII, n. 12, 36. Cited hereafter as *De matrimonio.*

11 Cf. Feije (1884), *De impedimentis et dispensationibus matrimonialibus* (Lovanii, 1874), pp. 99-100. Cited hereafter as *De impedimentis.*

12 *Theatrum veritatis et iustitiae* (16 vols., Coloniae Agrippinae, 1706), tom. III, pars II, disc. V *de matrimonio,* n. 28.

that any kind of a promise to marry was sufficient to exclude the impediment.[13]

The case of *raptus in parentes* remained the subject of controversy throughout the whole period in which the law of the Council of Trent was in force.[14] The more common opinion was that the impediment did not exist.[15] The proponents of each of the two contrasting opinions appealed to the decisions of the Sacred Congregation of the Council in support of their convictions. It seems that there was no decree of that Sacred Congregation so decisive as to be incapable of receiving an explanation in the terms of either view.

The earlier decisions, while not conclusive, tend rather to the severer opinion which admitted the presence of the impediment. This appears to be the obvious meaning of the celebrated decision of January 24, 1608.[16]

13 Cf. the *adnotationes Secretarii* in S.C.C., *Olomucen.*, 14 mart. 1772 — *Thesaurus resolutionum S. C. Concilii* (167 vols., Romae, 1718-1908), XLI, 60-61. This work will hereafter be cited thus: *Thesaurus.*

14 Cf. Feije, *De impedimentis,* p. 99.

15 Thus, e.g., De Iustis (fl. 1691), *De dispensationibus matrimonialibus tractatus* (Lucae, 1726), lib. II, c. XVIII, n. 56 sqq.; Reiffenstuel (+ 1703), *Ius canonicum universum* (ed. novissima, 6 vols. in 5, Romae, 1831-1834), lib. IV, tit. I, *de sponsalibus et matrimonio,* n. 20. The contrary opinion was held especially by Riganti (+ 1735), *Commentaria in regulas, constitutiones et ordinationes Cancellariae Apostolicae* (4 vols. in 2, Coloniae Allobrogum, 1751), in Reg. 49, n. 68 sqq.; and by the *Instructio pro iudiciis ecclesiasticis quoad causas matrimoniales,* n. 19 — *Acta et decreta sacrorum conciliorum recentiorum. Collectio Lacensis* (7 vols., Friburgi Brisgoviae, 1870-1890), V, col. 1288. This Instruction is in the main work of Cardinal Joseph Othmar de Rauscher (+ 1875). It is quite commonly referred to under the title Instructio Austriaca. It was promulgated, after its approval by a group of Roman theologians on May 4, 1855, along with the Austrian Concordat (Aug. 18, 1855).

16 The authenticity of this decree and its precise wording are attested by the Secretary of the Congregation in a communication under date of January 11, 1671. This letter is contained in Fessler (1872), "Ein Beitrag zum richtigen Verständniss des kirchlichen Ehehindernisses der Entführung *(raptus)*" — *AKKR,* VII (1862), 109-112. According to Feije *(De impedimentis,* p. 103) the letter was issued by the Secretary at the instigation of Cardinal De Luca for use in the Rota case of 1671 (cf. *infra,* pp. 24-25).

The dispositive part of this decree is as follows:

> . . . omnes (Cardinales) senserunt, Concilium procedere etiam in muliere volente, dum tamen sit raptus juxta terminos juris civilis.

Since the Roman law recognized the crime of *raptus in parentes,* this decision, on first reading, apparently offers a full confirmation of the existence of the impediment. It is, however, certain that the Council of Trent and the Sacred Congregation of the Council in several things did not intend to adopt the Roman law as regards abduction.[17] This decision is, therefore, better interpreted as envisioning especially the case of a girl who consented to the abduction but not to the marriage. In this case the impediment would have been present if she had been fraudulently induced to give the consent. The *votum* of an unnamed canonist, which has been transmitted along with the decision, confirms this interpretation.

It is worth noting, though, that this canonist hardly seems to have been opposed to the opinion which held the impediment to be present in the case of *raptus in parentes.* In fact, he cited with approval the opinion of Navarrus (1493-1586), and, by stating that the impediment would not be present if a woman *sui iuris* were abducted without violence or seduction, he implied that it would be present if she were not *sui iuris.*

A more convincing proof of the attitude of the Congregation in this period may be found in an undated decision which was transmitted in the same letter of 1671.[18] The case was that of a young woman under tutelage, who was carried off, *ad hoc tamen ea consentiente,* and then married by her abductor. The

17 E.g., the Sacred Congregation of the Council declared authoritatively on January 23, 1586, that only abduction for the purpose of marriage was included in the decree of the Council of Trent, even though the Roman law included abduction for any purpose under *raptus.* This decision is found in Gallemart (+ 1625), *Sacrosanctum oecumenicum Concilium Tridentinum, additis declarationibus Cardinalium Concilii Interpretum . . .* (Tridentini, 1737), in sess. XXIV, c. 6.

18 Cf. Fessler, *art. cit.,* p. 110.

guardian demanded the infliction of the Tridentine penalties. The Congregation replied as follows:

> Sacra Congregatio Cardinalium Concilii Tridentini interpretum censuit hujusmodi Raptorem secundum ea, quae proponuntur, comprehendi tam quoad poenas, quam quoad matrimonii prohibitionem decreto d. cap. 6, sess. 24. de reform. matrim.

The value of this response as an endorsement of the strict opinion depends, of course, on the precise force of the phrase *ad hoc tamen ea consentiente.* If this means that the woman consented to the abduction alone, the reply in no way endorses that view; but if it means that she consented to both the marriage and the abduction, then it definitely warrants that view.[19]

In the succeeding period it seems that the presence of the controversy caused the Curial officials to avoid any endorsement of one or the other view in the official documents. This is the net result which can be obtained from the lengthy case agitated in the Sacred Roman Rota from 1666 to 1671.[20] In several of its decisions on this case the Rota expressly endorsed the opinion which asserted the presence of the impediment when *raptus in parentes* had occurred, but it admitted that there was a doubt of law,[21] and the final decision (which declared the

19 A somewhat similar case from the diocese of Milan was solved in 1661 in an exactly opposite sense. In this case, however, the girl was legally betrothed to the man, although she had entered a formal petition for the dissolution of the engagement, and, despite this, had requested the abduction. The decision *"non constat (de raptu)"* could have been based on the existing betrothal. Cf. Gasparri, *Tractatus canonicus de matrimonio* (ed. altera, 2 vols., Paris, 1892), I, 379.

20 S. R. R., *Leodien., Nullitatis matrim.*, 28 iun. 1666 — *S. R. Rotae decisiones recentiores* (19 parts in 25 vols., Francofurti-Aureliae-Romae, 1623-1703), pars XIV, dec. 498; 27 ian. 1668 — *op. cit.*, pars XV, dec. 162; 22 iun., 1668 — *op. cit.*, pars XV, dec. 305; 13 iun. 1670 — *op. cit.*, pars XVI, dec. 250; 11 mart. 1671 — *op. cit.*, pars XVII, dec. 75. The decision of March 23, 1667 *(op. cit.*, pars XV, dec. 60), was merely the concession of a rehearing.

21 Cf., e.g., decision of March 23, 1667.

invalidity of the marriage in question) was not based at all on raptus, but on clandestinity.[22]

Two other decisions from approximately the same period show the prevalence of the strict view at Rome, although they are inconclusive since the final decision of the Congregation of the Council has not been transmitted. In both of these cases, one of which was from the diocese of Le Mans in France, and the other from Roermnod in Holland, a *votum* was presented by Cardinal Casaneti (+ 1700) in which the presence of the impediment of *raptus* was asserted inasmuch as the girl had been taken away without the knowledge of her father. In neither case did the Congregation give a decision on the question of the impediment. In the first case it ordered twice that further information be obtained, while in the second it instructed the Bishop to institute a juridical process on the nullity of the marriage.[23]

The unwillingness to decide the theoretical question was evidenced by the Congregation of the Council in a case from Ruvo di Puglia, Italy, decided in 1714.[24] In this case the *raptus,* if it had existed, had been purged by the separation of the woman from the abductor, but the Congregation ordered that the abductor was to be absolved *ad cautelam* from the penalties of *raptus* which had been declared by the Bishop. This *absolutio*

22 Cf. decision of March 11, 1671.

23 These cases are narrated in *Analecta iuris pontificii* (Romae, 1855-1868; Parisiis, 1869-1891), XXVIII (1888), col. 364-367. They date from the year 1681. It is surprising that Mitterer *(Geschichte,* p. 102) interprets these *vota* as part of the Congregation's decree.

24 S. C. C., *Ruben.,* 3 mart. 1714—Pallottini, *Collectio omnium conclusionum et resolutionum quae in causis propositis apud S. Cong. Cardinalium S. Concilii Tridentini Interpretum prodierunt ab anno 1564 ad annum 1860* (17 vols., Romae, 1868-1893), s. v. Matrimonium, XVIII, n. 25. The decision in this case is given erroneously *(censuit obesse* instead of *non obstare)* in *Codicis iuris canonici fontes cura Emi Petri Card. Gasparri editi* (9 vols., Romae et Civitate Vaticana: Typis Polyglottis Vaticanis, 1923-1939), n. 3131. This work will hereafter be cited thus: *Fontes.*

ad cautelam may be explained by the doubt of law which existed in the case of *raptus in parentes*.[25]

The canonists who denied the existence of the impediment in the case of *raptus in parentes* appealed especially to several decisions of the Congregation of the Council which date from a sowewhat later period. The first of these is a case from the diocese of Olmütz considered by the Congregation in 1769 and 1772.[26] The second time that this case was considered the argument revolved almost completely about the controversy on the impediment of abduction. The Cardinals decided that the invalidity of the marriage had not been sufficiently proved. Since the Congregation did not give the grounds for its decision, it is difficult to argue from this that therefore the Congregation denied the presence of the impediment. In fact, the woman in the case was alleged to have been engaged to the man, and this would have been sufficient grounds in that period for denying the invalidity of the marriage. Moreover, the very existence of the controversy rendered such a decision almost necessary, since the Congregation did not ordinarily decide questions of law in the course of a judicial trial.[27]

The same observations must be made in regard to the case considered in 1889.[28] Here again the absence of the impediment of *raptus* could have been declared because of the presence of true espousals as well as because of the fact that there existed

[25] Neither of the explanations proposed by Mitterer *(Geschichte*, p. 105) appears satisfactory. He suggests (a) that the absolution could have been enjoined in order to liberate the man from the penalties which the Bishop had inflicted in the external forum; (b) that the Congregation could have enjoined such an absolution in order to liberate itself from the necessity of getting more abundant information. The first suggéstion fails to explain why the absolution was given *ad cautelam*, since these penalties (in Mitterer's supposition, certainly invalid) were certainly existing in the external forum. The second explanation is rather contrary to the mode of acting of the Roman Congregations.

[26] S. C. C., *Olomucen.*, 29 iul. 1769 — *Thesaurus*, XXXIX, 60-72; 14 mart., 1772 — *Thesaurus*, XLI, 49-61.

[27] Wernz, *Ius Decretalium* (3 ed., 6 vols., Prati, 1913-1915), I, n. 146.

[28] S. C. C., *Aquen. seu Massilien.*, 16 febr. 1889 — *Thesaurus*, CXLVIII, 153-189.

in law no such impediment as that of *raptus in parentes.* The Congregation gave its decision in the usual form: the impediment of abduction had not been proved.

Some years previous to this, in fact, the severe opinion had been admitted as tenable when the Roman Curial officials approved as particular law for Austria the *Instruction* for procedure in marriage cases which had been written by Cardinal Rauscher (1797-1875). In this Instruction, appearing along with the Austrian Concordat in 1855, the existence of the impediment in the case of *raptus in parentes* was clearly asserted.[29]

It may be concluded, therefore, that the impediment was very doubtful, and therefore practically non-existent, in the case wherein a girl of minor age was abducted against the will of her parents but with her own consent, both to the marriage and to the abduction as a means thereto. There had been, however, no authoritative statement that the impediment was not present, and hence the opinion which asserted the impediment remained tenable. Practically, then, after the marriage had been contracted, a judge had little choice but to consider that no marriage could be declared invalid as long as the existence of any impediment to it was of a doubtful character. On the other hand, before the contraction of the marriage, the pastor had to assume the presence of the impediment and correspondingly had to implement its purgation before permitting the parties to exchange matrimonial consent in his presence.

29 *Instructio pro iudiciis ecclesiasticis quoad causas matrimoniales,* n. 19 — *Collectio Lacensis,* V, 1288.

Part Two

Canonical Commentary

INTRODUCTION

The present discipline of the Church in regard to the impediment of abduction is contained in canon 1074:

> **1. Inter virum raptorem et mulierem, intuitu matrimonii raptam, quandiu ipsa in potestate raptoris manserit, nullum potest consistere matrimonium.**
>
> **2. Quod si rapta, a raptore separata et in loco tuto ac libero constituta, illum in virum habere consenserit, impedimentum cessat.**
>
> **3. Quod ad matrimonii nullitatem attinet, raptui par habetur violenta retentio mulieris, cum nempe vir mulierem in loco ubi ea commoratur vel ad quem libere accessit, violenter intuitu matrimonii detinet.**

A comparison of the provisions of this canon with the pertinent chapter of session XXIV of the Council of Trent[1] immediately demonstrates a striking similarity between the two laws. Canon 1074, in fact, is a verbatim repetition of the provision of the Council with the addition of a few words. These additions are nothing more than the common doctrinal interpretation of the Tridentine decree.

There is one important exception. In the third paragraph the Code has settled a controversy which had been in existence for several centuries, and has assigned the effects of *raptus* to the case in which a woman was not carried off, but was merely detained in one place through violence.

1 Cf. *supra*, p. 18.

Aside from this provision, however, the Code is only a repetition of the legislation of the Council of Trent. Consequently the norm of interpretation to be followed in canon 1074 is given by canon 6, 2° and 3°. Insofar as canon 1074 agrees with the old law, it will be interpreted in accordance with that law, that is, in accord with the customary interpretation of that law by the approved authors. In those points in which it differs from the old law, it will be interpreted according to the proper meaning of its own terms, and hence according to the universal principles established in canons 17-19, in particular, those of canon 19.

A particular aid to the interpretation of the present canon is found in canon 2353.[2] This canon, while it is concerned with the crime of abduction as distinguished from the impediment, is certainly to be considered as a parallel provision of law. The clear distinction between the crime and the impediment of *raptus* in the Code will be of assistance in determining the proper concept of each. It must not, however, be supposed that they are identical institutes, that is, it cannot be admitted that canon 2353 is merely a penal sanction for the impediment contained in canon 1074. They are separate and distinct institutes, but they are very similar. In both canons the legislator speaks of *raptus,* and it must be assumed that the same fundamental concept underlies the word in both contexts, modified of course in each by the special qualities which the legislator has seen fit to add.

It will, nevertheless, be useful to insert here an outline of the principal differences between the impediment of abduction as contained in canon 1074, and the crime of abduction as made punishable in canon 2353. The crime, in one respect, has a much greater extension than the impediment, for the crime is committed if the woman is abducted either for marriage or for

2 Canon 2353: Qui intuitu matrimonii vel explendae libidinis causa rapuerit mulierem nolentem vi aut dolo, vel mulierem minoris aetatis consentientem quidem sed insciis vel contradicentibus parentibus aut tutoribus, ipso iure exclusus habeatur ab actibus legitimis ecclesiasticis et insuper aliis poenis pro gravitate culpae plectatur.

immoral purposes, while the impediment is not contracted unless the woman is carried off for the purpose of marriage. On the other hand, the impediment is incurred in the case of violent detention, whereas the text of canon 2353 makes no mention of detention, and hence, according to the general principles of penal law,[3] the crime cannot be said to have been committed in such a case. Finally, canon 1074 contains a provision whereby the parties may, of their own will, cause the invalidating effect to cease, but the punishment of the crime enacted in canon 2353 cannot be escaped except through the action of a legitimate ecclesiastical superior.

The present dissertation does not concern itself *ex professo* with the crime of *raptus*. The impediment is under consideration here, and the crime will be treated only incidentally.

The most difficult question in the interpretation of canon 1074 is the determination of the exact concept of *raptus*. The problem of the historical development of this institute has already been outlined. The many doubts which are connected with this evolution have had a certain reflex in the present day canonical interpretation; hence the necessity for some outline of the history. Nevertheless, the concept of *raptus* is now fairly well established and can, consequently, with some degree of accuracy be delineated.

3 Canon 2219, § 3.

CHAPTER IV

THE DEFINITION OF THE IMPEDIMENT

The Code of Canon Law does not present any formal definition of the impediment of abduction. Canon 1074 uses absolutely the words *raptor* and *rapta* without stating the exact extension of the two terms. Some elements, indeed, which are of help in the formation of the definition are presented in this canon. The other necessary properties will be supplied, in accord with what has already been said, from the old law and its interpretation through the approved authors.

A general definition of *raptus* has already been given. It is the forcible carrying off of a woman for the purpose of contracting marriage with her. There are therefore three elements which combine to form the impediment: (a) an abduction; (b) violence or force in connection with the abduction; (c) an intention of contracting marriage. Each of these will be treated separately.

ARTICLE I — THE ABDUCTION

Etymologically two distinct concepts are contained in the word *raptus:* an abduction or taking away, and violence connected therewith. The first of these necessarily implies some change of place, since a person or thing can hardly be said to have been abducted unless it has in some way been moved. For this reason the canonical authors in the period immediately following the Council of Trent unanimously held that some change of place was necessary in order that the impediment of *raptus* or abduction be verified.[1]

Change of place was necessary only in the sense that the woman actually had to be removed from the place where she

1 Cf., e.g., Navarrus (1493-1586), *Consilia seu responsa,* lib. V, tit. *de raptoribus,* cons. I.

was. It was not necessary that she be brought to the place where the abductor intended to keep her. The *raptus* was complete as soon as the woman was removed by a violent act of the abductor from the place in which she had been staying.[2]

In the succeeding centuries there was considerable discussion as to what precise change of place was necessary. Two distinct places were obviously necessary: the difficulty was in determining what physical distance was necessary in order that two places might properly be called distinct.[3] Insistence on the physical standard was gradually lessened in favor of a less material norm. The abduction had to be the transfer of a woman from a place where she was free from the influence of the abductor to a place where she was effectively under his power. The more common canonical opinion did not abandon entirely the physical norm, but used it together with the other as being complementary to it; any physical change of place, even that from room to room within the same house, was sufficient provided that thereby the woman was actually placed within the power of the abductor.[4]

The mere detention of a woman in her own home was not considered sufficient, according to the common opinion, to give rise to the impediment. Chiericato (+ 1717), however, taught that even this was enough, and a few later authors followed this opinion.[5] If a woman should have been detained in a place to which she had freely come, then a different problem was thereby

2 Cf. Guttierez (+ 1618), *Canonicae quaestiones* (3 vols., Noribergae-Lugduni, 1647-1661), tr. *de matrimonio*, c. 86, n. 13; Leurenius (1646-1723), *Forum ecclesiasticum* (3 vols., Venetiis, 1729), lib. IV, tit. I, cap. IX, q. CXXII, n. 8.

3 Cf. Ferraris (+ ca. 1763), *Bibliotheca canonica, iuridica, moralis, theologica, necnon ascetica, polemica, rubricistica, historica* (ed. novissima, 9 vols., Romae, 1885-1899), s.v. "Raptus"; De Justis (fl. 1691), *De dispensationibus matrimonialibus*, lib. II, c. XVIII, n. 66.

4 E.g., Leurenius, *Forum ecclesiasticum*, lib. IV, tit. I, cap. IX, q. CXXII, n. 8; Pichler (+ 1736), *Ius canonicum secundum quinque Decretalium titulos Gregorii Papae IX practice explicatum* (2 vols., Ravennae, 1741), lib. IV, tit. I, n. 117.

5 Chiericato's teaching is cited by Carrière (+ 1864) *(De matrimonio*, 2 vols., Parisiis, 1837, II, 165). Cf. also Feije, *De impedimentis*, p. 97.

presented, for there was indeed some change of place, even though it had not been caused by the abductor. Consequently Billuart (1685-1757) held that this was at least a virtual abduction.[6] The majority of the canonists however continued to insist that an actual change of place caused by the abductor had to take place in order that the impediment be incurred.[7]

A practical solution has been given to these controversies by the provision of canon 1074, §3. The legislator has there decreed that the forcible detention of a woman in her own home or at a place to which she has freely come is to be considered as equivalent to abduction so far as the invalidity of the marriage is concerned. The juridic effects of abduction and of violent detention are therefore exactly the same as regards marriage, and they will consequently be treated together in this present dissertation except where the subject matter itself demands otherwise.[8]

It is to be carefully observed that the mere fact of abduction or of violent detention does not give rise to any impediment to marriage. It is necessary that by this fact the woman be reduced to the power of the abductor and that she remain in his

6 *Summa Sancti Thomae hodiernis academiarum moribus accommodata* (ed. nova, 8 vols., Parisiis-Romae-Bruxellis, 1880-1900), tr. *de temperantia,* diss. VI, art. IV, § II.

7 Schmalzgrueber (+ 1735), *Ius ecclesiasticum universum* (12 vols., Romae, 1843-1845), lib. V, tit. XVII, n. 4; Wernz, *Ius decretalium* IV, n. 280. Gasparri (*Tractatus canonicus de matrimonio* [1892], I, n. 557) remained doubtful on this point.

8 The exact terminology to be used in regard to violent detention has been the subject of a rather unimportant disagreement among the canonical authors. Mitterer and several others maintain that the forcible detention of a woman is a new impediment distinct from that of abduction (*raptus*). Other canonists, e.g., Wernz-Vidal, consider it as a second form of the impediment of abduction. Cf. Mitterer, *Geschichte,* p. 94; Wernz-Vidal, *Ius canonicum,* tom. V: *Ius matrimoniale* (ed. altera, Romae, 1928), n. 308.

It is, of course, true that the violent detention of a woman is not properly included under the impediment of abduction, and likewise that the Code distinguished between violent detention and *raptus,* but the close similarity of the two institutes gives good reason for treating them as forms of the same impediment.

power. Thus this impediment differs completely in its workings from the impediment of crime, even though both have their origin in a criminal act. By the placing of the criminal act of spouse-murder or of adultery with the necessary concomitant circumstances the impediment of crime arises and it will cease only through legitimate dispensation. Abduction, on the other hand, exists only if the woman has by the criminal act of abduction or detention been placed in the power of the man,[9] and it ceases as soon as she is released from his power in accord with the provisions of the law. The criminal act of abduction or detention is necessary as a pre-requisite, but it does not give rise to the impediment unless the woman is actually held in the power of the man.

There are therefore two essential acts in the impediment: a criminal act of abduction or of violent detention and a subsequent retention of the woman under the power of the man. It is, of course, necessary that these two be intimately connected, so that the retention is the result of the criminal act. Abduction and violent detention are essentially acts by which the woman is placed under the influence of the abductor or detainer *(in potestate raptoris).*[10] The Code does not define the *potestas raptoris,* but it declares the conditions under which it ceases.[11] These conditions — separation from the abductor and the placing of the woman in a safe and secure place — must both be fulfilled before the impediment will cease. Thus the impediment (and the power of the abductor) remains even though the woman is free and safe in a given place so long as she is not actually separated from the abductor. The power of the abductor there-

9 Knecht (+ 1932), *Handbuch des katholischen Eherechts* (Freiburg im Breisgau: Herder, 1928), p. 446.

10 Gasparri, *Tractatus canonicus de matrimonio* (ed. nova ad mentem Codicis I. C., 2 vols. in 1, Typis Polyglottis Vaticanis, 1932), I, n. 645; Farrugia, *De matrimonio et causis matrimonialibus,* (Taurini-Romae: Marietti, 1924), n. 182. This edition of Cardinal Gasparri's work will hereafter be quoted thus: *De matrimonio.*

11 Canon 1074, §2. From §1 of the same canon it is evident that the impediment and the power of the abductor are so connected that when the one ceases the other likewise fails. Cf. *infra,* pp. 74-80.

fore comes into existence by means of a violent act, but it can continue in existence despite the cessation of the violence. Violence is consequently not a necessary component of the state which is called in the Code the *potestas raptoris*.[12]

This is of particular importance as regards the impediment of violent detention. According to the Code violent detention has exactly the same consequences in the matter of the validity of a subsequent marriage as abduction *(raptus)*. Now the Code expressly declares that abduction renders a marriage invalid only if this marriage is contracted while the abducted woman remains in the power of her abductor. For the impediment of violent detention, then, the marriage will likewise be invalid only if it takes place while she is in his power. Therefore even if the woman is no longer violently retained, she cannot contract marriage until the conditions of canon 1074, §2, have been fully satisfied. The mere cessation of violence is not enough: she must also be separated from the man who detained her, and in addition be established in a safe and free place.[13]

It is not necessary that the woman be confined in a single room or house in order that the impediment of abduction or violent detention be verified. The size of the place where she is confined is immaterial.[14] She may, in fact, be permitted considerable freedom of movement, and be brought from place to place, provided she is kept under constant surveillance to prevent her escape from the influence of the abductor or detainer.[15]

12 Gasparri, *De matrimonio*, I, n. 650. The contrary opinion is expressed by Muniz, *Procedimientos ecclesiasticos* (2 ed., 3 vols., Sevilla, 1926), II, 349; and by Falco, *Corso di diritto ecclesiastico* (Padova: Milani, 1930), p. 205.

13 Schönsteiner, *Grundriss des kirchlichen Eherechts* (2. Aufl., Wien: Auer, 1937), p. 369; Knecht, *Handbuch*, p. 448. Augustine (+ 1943) implies that violence is a necessary component of violent detention throughout the whole time that the impediment exists. Cf. *A Commentary on the New Canon Law*, Vol. V: *Marriage Laws and Matrimonial Trials* (4 rev. ed., St. Louis and London: Herder, 1929), p. 195.

14 Cappello, *Tractatus canonico-moralis de sacramentis*, Vol. III, *De matrimonio* (4 ed., 2 toms., Taurinorum Augustae: Marietti, 1939), I, n. 461.

15 S. C. C., *Herbipolen.*, 24 apr. 1858 — *Fontes*, n. 4162.

No special characteristic need be present, either in the place from which she is abducted, or in the place to which she is taken, beyond the fact that in the first she is not under the power of the abductor, while in the second she is effectively reduced to that power. Thus it is inaccurate to say that the abduction must be from a safe place, as most authors require.[16] The abduction may be from a place which is not safe for the woman concerned, e. g., from the power of another abductor.[17] Similarly the statement that a woman cannot be held in her own home under the influence of the abductor is not precisely accurate.[18] It is, in fact, quite conceivable that a man could forcibly take a girl from the more public part of her own home into a remoter section with the intention of keeping her there until she consented to marry him. In this case all of the conditions for a violent abduction would be fulfilled and the impediment would be present. The *terminus ad quem* of a violent abduction might easily be the home of the abducted person if she were seized away from it, especially if the parents of the woman were in connivance with the abductor. Finally, it is quite possible that a woman could be detained for such a purpose within the limits of her own home, either by the abductor himself or by the woman's parents acting as the agents of a favored suitor.

Article II — The Necessary Violence

The second essential element of *raptus* is violence. Three questions require attention in regard to this violence. These are: (a) what is to be understood under the term *violence* in this connection; (b) at what stage in the abduction must this violence be present; (c) against whom must it be used.

16 Cappello, *De matrimonio,* I, n. 460; Wernz-Vidal, *Ius matrimoniale,* n. 369.

17 Payen *(De matrimonio in missionibus ac potissimum in Sinis tractatus practicus et casus,* 2a ed., 3 vols., Zi-ka-wei: T'ou-se'-we', 1936, I, n. 1297) posits such a case.

18 Triebs (+ 1942), *Praktisches Handbuch des geltenden kanonischen Eherechts in Vergleichung mit dem deutschen staatlichen Eherecht* (Breslau: Ostdeutsche Verlagsanstalt, 1933), p. 354.

A. Comprehension of the term violence

Violence may be defined, in accord with the classical definition, as an impetus from without compelling the object against which it is directed to do or suffer something contrary to its internal inclination.[19] It is divided into absolute violence and relative or moral violence. The former is that violence which is fully resisted but without success; the latter, that which could have been at least partially resisted with success. The idea of fear is intimately connected with that of moral violence. Indeed, some authors define moral violence simply as the inflicting of fear.[20] More properly, the relation of the two may be expressed thus: moral violence is the immediate or foreseen danger of some evil which causes an agitation of the mind; fear is this very perturbation of the mind caused by the perception or foresight of an evil.[21]

Physical violence affects directly the external faculties of man: it does not enter the will at all, and consequently the act which is performed under the influence of physical violence does not proceed from the will and cannot be called voluntary. The will is not coerced by physical violence; it is simply precluded from making a human choice. Moral violence however causes a mental perturbation which results in a true coercion of the will. The will is moved to action because of the evil which it perceives imminent or proximate. The freedom of the will is diminished, and therefore the person is said to have acted unwillingly, even though, as a matter of fact, the will has chosen this action deliberately as the lesser of two evils.

19 "Vis est motio cuius principium est extra in contrarium renitente eo qui patitur"—Vermeersch (+ 1936), *Theologia moralis* (3. ed., 4 vols., Romae: Pont. Università Gregoriana, 1933-1937), I, n. 71. Cf. Sangmeister, *Force and Fear as Precluding Matrimonial Consent* (The Catholic University of America Canon Law Studies, n. 80, Wash., D. C.: The Catholic University of America, 1932), pp. 5-7.

20 Cf., e. g., Feije, *De impedimentis*, p. 81; Ayrinhac-Lydon, *Marriage Legislation in the New Code of Canon Law* (New York: Benziger Brothers, 1940), p. 205.

21 Gasparri, *De matrimonio*, II, n. 832.

Since the primary interest of the Church in her legislation on the impediment of abduction has been to insure as far as possible the complete freedom of the woman to marry whom she will, both physical and moral violence, are, in the unanimous opinion of the authors who comment on the pre-Code law, sufficient to cause an impediment of abduction.[22] The post-Code commentators, too, agree in admitting that moral violence is enough to give rise to the impediment.[23]

In a recent book, however, Köstler states that the opinion which denies the necessity of physical violence is erroneous. His argument is taken from the equality which the third paragraph of canon 1074 establishes between *raptus* and *retentio*. Since the retention is qualified as violent, this equality established in the law requires that the *raptus* also be violent. In the Code violence is, moreover, distinguished from fear and intrigue (cc. 103; 542, §1). Therefore the kind of violence whose presence must be presupposed for the existence of this impediment is not really perpetrated, and consequently not present in a case, when the circumstances connote nothing more than an interplay of fear, intrigue, or flattery.[24]

It is not difficult to reply to this argument in so far as it concerns the actual abduction (as distinguished from the violent detention) and the inclusion of fear as giving rise to the impediment.[25] Canon 1074, §3, in fact, establishes no equality between *raptus* and *retentio* except insofar as their effect on marriage is concerned. The terms of reference, moreover, are not

22 Santi- (+ 1885) Leitner (+ 1929), *Praelectiones iuris canonici* (5 vols. in 3, Ratisbonae-Romae-Neo Eboraci-Cincinnatii: Pustet, 1895), lib. IV, tit. I, n. 155; Wernz, *Ius Decretalium,* IV, n. 280.

23 Cf., e.g., Vermeersch-Creusen, *Epitome iuris canonici* (3 vols., Mechlinae-Romae, vol. I, 6 ed., 1936, vols. II-III, 5 ed., 1934-1936), II, n. 330; Triebs, *Praktisches Handbuch,* p. 352; Cappello, *De matrimonio,* I, n. 465.

24 *Das österreichische Konkordats-Eherecht* (Wien: Springer, 1937), p. 61, note 2. Köstler does not speak of moral and physical violence in these terms, but he excludes moral violence by denying that fear, intrigue, or flattery will suffice to give rise to the impediment.

25 For a consideration of the impediment as arising from intrigue and flattery, cf. *infra,* pp. 41-53.

raptus and *retentio* simply, but *raptus* and *violenta retentio*. It is therefore illogical to maintain that the same kind of violence is required by the law for both. The requirement of violence in §1 is deduced from the word *raptus* itself, which, as Köstler himself notes, includes the idea of violence. The species of violence required will be determined not by its comparison with other texts of the present law; but by the traditional concept of the word in canonical thought and in the old law. There is no evidence that the legislator has desired through the Code to effect a change in the traditional understanding of the word *raptus*.

Köstler's argument constitutes a more serious difficulty when it is restricted to the case of a violent detention of a woman for marriage. Here indeed there is a positive requirement of violence for a particular species of the impediment which exists as new legislation. It is therefore to be interpreted according to its own sense, and not from the old law.[26]

It is true, of course, that the Code of Canon Law constantly distinguishes *vis, metus,* and *dolus,*[27] and that the word *violentia,* aside from the present instance, seems to be used by the Code in designation of physical violence only.[28] The word *raptus,* however, in canon 1074, §1, implies violence and is to be understood of moral violence in accord with the traditional teaching. The context of canon 1074, §3, therefore, or at least the parallel provision of canon 1074, §1, seems to require that the violence there mentioned be understood as including moral along with physical violence. The purpose of the law, too, requires this interpretation. The impediment is intended for the protection of the liberty of the woman, which is equally endangered through a detention which is accomplished through moral violence and one which takes place with physical violence. The purpose of the impediment of violent retention is obviously the same as that of the impediment of abduction. Consequently the kind of violence

26 Canon 6, §3.

27 Canons 103; 542, §1; 572, §1. The combination *vis et metus* is of even more frequent occurrence: cf., e.g., canons 1087, §1; 1095, §1; 3°; etc.

28 Canons 2343, §1; 2354, §1. Cf. Köstler, *Wörterbuch zum Codex Iuris Canonici* (München: Kösel-Pustet, 1927-1929), s.v. "violentia, violentus."

presupposed in either case is one and the same. It may therefore be concluded that moral violence is sufficient to give rise to the impediment of *raptus* and the cognate impediment of violent detention.

The meaning of the term *moral violence* has been explained above, but it is now necessary to investigate the content of this expression in its particular application to the impediment. This term has been very widely accepted in this connection, and the limits to which it should be extended are still a matter of controversy.

According to modern teaching the characteristic note of the moral violence which is required for giving rise to this impediment is to be found in the fact that the woman is unwilling. The abduction or detention must be against the will of the victim.[29] It proceeds, therefore, primarily from the will of someone else. Now, this may come about entirely and completely against the will of the person who is abducted without any concurring act of her will at all, as, for example, when absolute physical violence is employed, or when the victim is hypnotized, or so frightened that the will cannot act with any deliberation or consent at all. In all of these cases, of course, there is enough violence to cause the impediment.[30]

On the other hand this unwillingness may consist not merely in an inability to act but also in a reluctance for placing the act. The person is said to be unwilling, even though, in fact, she does place the act, because she places it only because of the violence of the man abducting her. She concurs in the abduction because of the moral violence of the other person. Her concurrence is, therefore, a *voluntarium simpliciter* and an *involun-*

[29] Cf., e.g., S. Alphonsus Maria de Ligorio (+ 1787), *Theologia moralis* (ed. nova cura et studio P. L. Gaudé, 4 vols., Romae: Typis Polyglottis Vaticanis, 1905-1912), lib. VI, n. 1107; Prümmer (+ 1931), *Manuale theologiae moralis* (ed. octava, 3 vols., Friburgi Brisgoviae: Herder, 1936), III, n. 820; Wernz-Vidal, *Ius matrimoniale*, n. 312.

[30] Wernz-Vidal, *Ius matrimoniale*, p. 370 (cf. p. 581); Prümmer, *Manuale theologiae moralis*, III, n. 820.

tarium secundum quid.[31] The moral violence of the abductor, then, is the act or actions by which the reluctance of the victim is overcome and she is induced to concur in the abduction.

Properly considered such moral violence exists only when the actions of the man cause a disturbance of the will, i.e., when the will itself is coerced; in other words, when fear is inflicted. Moral violence in this sense is certainly sufficient to give rise to the impediment, for this has been the common understanding of the word violence in this connection both before and since the Code.[32] Such violence would be inflicted on the woman through serious threats, for example, or in any other way which would cause grave fear. The same norms will be used for estimating the gravity necessary for this impediment as in determining what fear invalidates a marriage because of defective consent.[33] There is general agreement that grave fear is required, although some few authors do not specify the gravity as being necessary.[34]

A limitation of the freedom of the individual may take place also through the use of fraud and intrigue. While fear affects directly the will of the person, fraud and intrigue affect the will only indirectly through the intellect. Notwithstanding this, since the will cannot act except on the basis of the data provided by the intellect, the use of fraud and deceit effectively diminishes the voluntariness of the act. Hence it has become a fairly common opinion that fraud and intrigue *(dolus malus)*, as the equivalent of moral violence, are sufficient to give rise to the impediment of abduction and detention.

The history of this opinion is very involved. It is connected with the long dispute on *raptus seductionis* and with the opinion which asserted the presence of the impediment when no real abduction had occurred, but there was merely the detention of a woman in one place. It is connected with the former inasmuch

31 Cf. Merkelbach, *Summa theologiae moralis* (3 vols., Parisiis: Desclée, Vols. I-II, ed. 3a, 1938; Vol. III, ed. 2a, 1936), I, n. 73.

32 Cf. *supra*, pp. 37-38.

33 Cf. Mitterer, *Geschichte*, p. 96.

34 E.g., Petrovits, *The New Church Law on Matrimony* (2nd ed., Philadelphia: McVey, 1926), p. 215.

as fraud and intrigue entered frequently into the seduction by means of which *raptus* was alleged to be present. The present impediment of violent detention includes most of the cases which were formerly considered to be *raptus* because of intrigue.

In the classical period of Canon Law there was a definite division of opinion on this question. One opinion, possibly the more common one, denied that *dolus* was sufficient to give rise to the impediment.[35] The contrary view was, however, taken by a good many authors.[36] Since 1864 the latter opinion had been almost universally accepted. The reason for this is that in that year the Sacred Congregation of the Council considered a case from the Archdiocese of Paris in which the woman had been brought through intrigue into the power of the man and was detained by him for the purpose of extorting her consent to marriage. The woman had been under the surveillance of a maid-servant who was acting in collusion with the man. On the 25th of June, the Congregation declared the marriage invalid, and on the 27th of August it confirmed this decision.[37]

The argument in the case turned not only on the question of *raptus* but also on that of *vis et metus*. The advocate of the woman asserted the presence of the impediment of abduction, because (1) there had been violence against the *patriapotestas* of the father; (2) because the woman had been abducted through *dolus;* (3) because there had been true and patent violence in the case. Furthermore, he contended, even if this impediment were not admitted, the marriage was null because of force and fear. The Defender of the Bond, of course, attempted to answer

35 Sanchez, *De matrimonio,* lib. VII, disp. XIII, n. 12; Schmalzgrueber, *Ius ecclesiasticum universum,* lib. V, tit. XVII, n. 29; Leurenius, *Forum ecclesiasticum,* lib. IV, tit. I, cap. IX, III, q. CXXII, n. 10; La Croix (+ 1714), *Theologia moralis* (3 vols., Ravennae, 1761), lib. VI, pars III, n. 633.

36 E.g., De Iustis, *De dispensationibus matrimonialibus,* lib. II, c. XVIII, n. 69; Pyrrhus (+ 1686), *Praxis dispensationum apostolicarum* (Neapoli, 1641), lib. VII, cap. VI, n. 55.

37 Cf. the report of the case in *Analecta iuris pontificii* (VII [1864], 1108-1116) which is more complete than that contained in *Acta Sanctae Sedis* (41 vols., Romae, 1865-1908), I, 15-23. The *Acta Sanctae Sedis* will hereafter be cited by the symbol *ASS.*

all of these propositions, denying in particular that abduction through fraud and intrigue was sufficient to constitute *raptus*. The Congregation, according to its usual wont, gave no grounds for its decision.

Cardinal D'Annibale (+ 1892), who wrote but a few years (1871-1873) after this decision, considered this case as having been decided on the grounds of force and fear. Consequently he taught that the impediment of abduction did not arise from the use of fraud and intrigue.[38] Vecchiotti (+ 1870), at about the same time, stated that it was a case of violent detention, and cited it to support his theory that violent detention gave rise to the impediment if the woman had actually been called to the place where she was detained. In other words, as long as there was a change of place, the impediment was verified.[39]

The editor of the *Acta Sanctae Sedis*, however, considered the solution of the case as implying an authoritative statement that the impediment of abduction existed when a woman had been brought into the man's power through fraud and intrigue. In his conclusions from this case he established the following principles: (a) to betray a girl by fraud so that she comes unknowingly into the hands of a man who intends violence is the same as to abduct her forcibly from her own home; (b) it is immaterial whether the girl did or did not consent to these frauds, for consent obtained by fraud is the equivalent of open violence.[40]

These conclusions have strongly influenced the teaching of the modern canonists. They have in fact been accepted by many authors without any substantial change.[41] There are several

38 *Summula theologiae moralis* (ed. 4a, 3 vols., Romae, 1879), pars III, n. 446, nota 29.

39 Cf. *Institutiones canonicae ex operibus Ioannis Card. Soglia excerptae* (16 ed., 3 vols., Augustae Taurinorum, 1876), III, 236.

40 *ASS*, I (1865-1866), 23-24.

41 Gasparri, *De matrimonio*, I, 647; Mansella, *De impedimentis matrimonium dirimentibus ac de processu iudiciali in causis matrimonialibus notiones et disceptationes canonicae* (Romae, 1881), p. 16; Nau (+ 1935), *Manual on the Marriage Laws of the Code of Canon Law* (2nd ed., New York-Cincinnati: Pustet, 1934), p. 99.

important canonists, however, who limit the impediment to those cases in which the woman is not only unaware of the abductor's intentions, but also unwilling. Thus, for example, Wernz-Vidal say, "Violence can be exercised . . . also through fraud by which an unwilling girl is fraudulently betrayed when, that is, not knowing in what direction the matter tends, she does not consent to the frauds which are betraying her."[42]

The following case will illustrate the difference between the two opinions: With marriage in view, but without revealing this intention to her, Cyrus invites Julia to visit him in his summer home on the pretext of recreation. He detains her there by flattery and finally tells her of his desire for marriage with her. She gives her consent willingly.[43]

According to the first opinion there is an impediment of abduction: the girl has been abducted fraudulently, since she did not know the intention of the abductor. In the second opinion there is no impediment, unless she objected to the fraud which was used to bring her to the place where the proposal was made.[44] The impediment is not present because there has been no violence.

For most cases in which *dolus* is employed, the Code provides a practical solution in canon 1074, §3, by introducing the new species of the impediment of *raptus:* violent detention. When fraud and intrigue are used to bring the woman into the man's power, violence of another sort will usually be employed to detain her. In the case as outlined above, though, there is no violence at all except that which is evidenced by the fraud used to

42 *Ius matrimoniale*, n. 312; cf. also note 21: "iste dolus aequiparatur violentiae, si puella inscia fuit quo res tenderent, nec fraudibus illis consensit et a fraudibus sese extricare non potuit." The same opinion is held by Cappello, *De matrimonio*, I, n. 465; Aertnys (+1915)-Damen, *Theologia moralis* (13a ed., 2 vols., Taurini-Romae: Marietti, 1939), II, n. 733; and others.

43 Matharan (+ 1894), *Casus de matrimonio* (Parisiis-Matriti, 1893), p. 205, casus 236.

44 It is not easy to understand what is meant by objection to the fraud, or correlatively in what consent to the fraud would consist. Cf. *infra*, p. 46.

bring to a place where the man can exert an influence. The dispute which exists among the canonical authorities imposes, in this case, a solution, at least in the practical order, in favor of the restrictive interpretation of the law, for such a controversy indicates that the application of the law is doubtful.[45] Hence the impediment exists only when a woman is fraudulently abducted against her will: she must not only be unaware of the abductor's intent to marry, but also be unwilling in that intention.

This solution seems to accord better, too, with the common doctrine on the violence which is necessary for the impediment. In fact, the characteristic note of this violence is the reluctance of the woman. Now, in the case under discussion, at the moment that the woman comes into the power of the man, there can hardly be question of any such reluctance in a proper sense, since the woman places the act without knowledge of the abductor's intention. She is willing in the act which she places, and that act is not, as in the case of fear, a *volutarium simpliciter* and an *involuntarium secundum quid.* It is a fully voluntary act. The consequences of her act, however, may be so repugnant to her will that, were she in possession of full knowledge, the act would not be placed. This will be true only if the woman actually rejects those consequences, in other words, if she is really unwilling in the act so far as it involves the abductor's intention. If she is instead willing to accept these consequences, there is no real reluctance, and consequently no violence, even in the extended sense in which the word is used here. It is to be noted that the concern of her unwillingness needs to be referable only to the abduction or the intrigue. The while she is not unwilling to marry the man, she does object to the means used by him. This situation would suffice to give rise to the impediment. When the woman is merely unaware of the man's intention without objecting to it, then no violence is sustained by her despite the fact that it may be intended by the man. In such a case there is not actual, but only an intentional violence. In other

45 Can. 15. Moreover the restrictive interpretation is also required by the principles enunciated in canons 19 and 1035.

words, the violence has not become a perpetrated fact, but at the most exists only as a projected act which still needs execution if it is to be brought within the realm of juridical actuality.

Subsequent consent to whatever fraud was employed will not suffice to preclude the rise of the impediment. If at the moment the woman comes into the power of the man, she is actually unwilling to be brought in this manner under the man's power, the violence necessary for the rise of the impediment seems to be already verified, and subsequent consent would not be enough for the cessation of the impediment. It is difficult to understand what is meant by consent to the fraud if this consent is supposed as being co-existent with the fraud itself. If the woman knows of the attendant act of intrigue, then she cannot really be considered a victim of it. If instead she only suspects the intrigue and yet does nothing to avoid or obviate it, then the impediment will exist, if, through such fraud, she is unwillingly, i.e., contrary to her will, brought into the man's power. It will not exist if she is not unwilling. Her refusal or even her non-concern to extricate herself from the man's intrigue is culpable, and will be an indication that she is willingly abducted, but it cannot effect the preclusion of the impediment if real violence is actually present.

Finally, the case decided in 1864 may be adduced in favor of this interpretation of the impediment. It was concerned with a woman who was actually not only unaware of the man's intention when she came into his power, but who was very definitely opposed to it. Since this case seems to be the only foundation in law or in jurisprudence for the assertion that fraud and intrigue suffice for the impediment, it is certainly better to limit to the actual data there presented whatever conclusions one may rightly derive therefrom.

In the present day law of the Church, however, it does not seem necessary to admit that the impediment of abduction can be incurred through an abduction in which intrigue alone is used to bring the woman under the power of the man. The cases which, under the former law, led to the introduction of this opinion concerning intrigue were those in which a woman had been invited on some pretext to come to a place where the man then forcibly detained her for the purpose of marriage.[46] These cases constituted a true difficulty under the old law inasmuch as that legislation envisaged only *raptus,* which was essentially a carrying off. The new law, however, has introduced another form of the impediment: violent detention. The cases which were included under abduction through intrigue in the old legislation will now be considered cases of violent detention.

In regard to this set of cases, then, there has been a change of law: the new law is contained in canon 1074, §3. Consequently an abduction through intrigue alone will give rise to the impediment only insofar as it involves a detention of the woman through physical or true moral violence (fear).

This interpretation is confirmed by a comparison of canon 1074 with canon 2353. Canon 1074 has no mention of the means by which moral violence can be inflicted, but makes violent detention an impediment. On the other hand, canon 2353 does not allude to violent detention at all, but mentions *dolus* as one of the means of abducting the woman.[47] Hence both canons cover much the same ground, but do so in different ways. Canon 2353 has retained the old law, while canon 1074 has extended the provision of the old law and reduced it to a more coherent system. There is, however, no equivalency established between the two canons in regard to the abduction through intrigue. Canon 1074 includes under violent detention many cases which will not be punished by canon 2353 as abduction through intrigue. Thus, e.g., a woman may be detained in her own home by the man: ordinarily in this case there will be no intrigue used to induce her to come to the place, but there will be moral violence employed to keep her there. There is no crime of abduction through intrigue, but there is an impediment of violent detention. Contrariwise canon 2353 includes as abduction through intrigue some cases which will not give rise to the impediment.

46 Cf., e.g., De Iustis (fl. 1691), *De dispensationibus matrimonialibus,* lib. II, c. XVIII, n. 69; Pyrrhus (+ 1686), *Praxis dispensationum apostolicarum,* lib. VII, c. VI, n. 55.

47 Canon 2353: "Qui . . . rapuerit mulierem nolentem vi aut dolo . . ."

Thus, even if one abstracts from the question of the difference of intention required for the crime and for the impediment, those cases in which the woman is brought by intrigue to a place but is not violently detained there will constitute the crime of abduction, but will not give rise to the impediment.

The force of the argument which is taken from the comparison of canon 1074 with canon 2353 is increased if some attention is given to the reason which underlies the two different provisions. Canon 2353 is equal in extension to the old law; the penalties for *raptus* have been made much milder, but it is precisely the same cases which were punished under the old law that are now comprehended. The legislator has abstained from extending the penalty since the crime is now of comparatively rare occurrence, and the public good does not require that the Church use her penalties to extirpate it. Hence the former extension of the law was considered sufficient.

Canon 1074, on the other hand, has a much greater extension than the preceding law, for it includes not only *raptus*, but also the detention of a woman in the place where she lives or in a place to which she has freely come. The reason for this extension of the old law is easy to understand. The impediment is not a penal provision; it is designed to protect the liberty of the woman concerned. Now this reason obtains, even urgently so, despite the comparative rarity of abduction or detention for the purpose of marriage. Hence the Church has extended her laws to include all cases in which the woman's freedom is endangered.

A consideration of the consequences of the opinion which admits intrigue as sufficient to give rise to the impediment of abduction or of violent detention also persuades acceptance of the contrary view. For it must be remembered that, if there is question of a case in which intrigue has been used to bring the woman into the man's power, decisive importance attaches to the moment in which the woman discovers that she has been deceived. Until that moment arrives, the woman has not suffered any violence; she has willingly accompanied the man, even though her willingness is based on an erroneous belief. The unwillingness of which there is question in a case of intrigue really refers rather to the consequences of her act. If she had known of the consequences, she would not have placed the act. Yet as a matter of fact the act has been placed willingly. In the moment in which the woman discovers that she has been deceived, however, she is at liberty to approve of that action or to reject it. If she approves of it, there can be no question of an impediment of abduction, for her abduction or detention is entirely in accord with her will, and there cannot be any question of true violence.[48] If she rejects that action and now desires that it would not have been placed because of the consequences which she sees coming from it, she is now able to avoid those consequences. For the man, in the terms of the present case, is using no violence to force her to stay with him or to marry him. She is at liberty to go. If she chooses to stay with the man, she can hardly be said to have come into his power as a result of his violent action.

If the man should again use intrigue to detain the woman in his power, the same difficulty would arise.[49] For in this case, too, the important moment will be that in which the woman learns of the man's deceit. If she does not learn of this deceit until after the marriage, the validity of the marriage will be determined according to the norms of canon 1083, that is, according to the general canonical principles on error. There is no special reason why the woman who has gone along with the man and has not separated from him should be protected from the results of such an error, while a woman who would have wanted to be beyond the power of the man would nevertheless be constrained by law to remain in the marriage, were it to be contracted. The purpose of the law would seem to require the same provision in both cases.[50] Furthermore it would almost be im-

48 Cf. *supra*, pp. 45-46.

49 It is of course obvious that, if the man leads the woman to believe that some calamity will come upon her if she leaves him, there is real moral violence. Such a belief could be engendered by fraud, but this fraud itself would be a means of producing real fear. In such a case there would be an impediment of violent abduction or detention because of the use of true moral violence.

50 There does not seem to be any reason for attaching a decisive im-

possible in practice to determine whether or not the intrigue which was used actually resulted in reducing the woman to the man's power. Detention of the woman through intrigue certainly is very similar to the use of intrigue to extort marital consent.

The acknowledgement of intrigue as one of the means of inflicting moral violence seems to be unnecessary and confusing. It is unnecessary because the woman's liberty is well protected if the impediment of abduction is produced only by the employment of real moral violence, that is, of fear. It is confusing because it would lead to innumerable practical difficulties in determining the state of mind of the woman at the moment in which she became aware of the man's deceit. For there will be no external influence of the man from which to judge; the judgment would depend ultimately on the subjective state of mind and will in the woman.

Since, therefore, the opinion which admits *dolus* as sufficient for giving rise to the impediment can adduce only one disputed decision to support its claim, it does not appear temerarious to resume the classical opinion, and to state that only physical or moral violence can give rise to the impediment of abduction or detention. Consequently the present writer is in agreement with the conclusion of Köstler which has already been mentioned. *Dolus* of itself will not give rise to the impediment of abduction.

There is a third way, according to some authors, in which the will of the woman may be influenced and moral violence inflicted upon her. This is the case of the so-called *raptus seductionis,* that is, when the man obtains the consent of the woman through gifts, promises, flattery, importunate entreaties, and the like. It is extremely important in this matter to place the question in its proper terms: much of the confusion which is found in the modern treatment of this impediment seems to stem from a failure to distinguish well the precise amplitude of this question and its relation to the alleged impediment of *raptus in parentes.*

portance to the new juridical element which is introduced by the fact that the man has through fraud brought the woman to a new place.

First of all, the present discussion is not concerned with those cases in which these devices (gifts, etc.) are used as a means of inflicting fear or of deceiving the woman. It is quite generally taught that *preces importunae* can, when joined with reverential fear and with threats, cause fear sufficiently grave to render a marriage invalid because of defect of consent.[51] Such entreaties would also give rise to the impediment of abduction, but not precisely because of the *preces* themselves, but rather because of the fear inflicted.[52] Similarly these arts may all be used as a means of bringing the woman into the power of the man without her knowledge of his intention of obtaining marriage. In such a case it is the deception involved which occupies the important place, and the impediment will be present or absent accordingly as one admits or rejects the opinion which admits *dolus* to be enough to effect the impediment.[53]

There is no question here of the alleged irrebuttable presumption *(iuris et de iure)* that these arts have been employed when a woman under twenty-five years of age has been willingly abducted for marriage without parental consent. No proof or evidence can be offered to establish the existence or juridical validity of such a presumption in Canon Law at the present. This presumption was introduced by a few authors[54] as an aid towards establishing whether the impediment was present when the violence in question was that which was employed against the parents.

The present discussion, therefore, concerns only the case in which simply such devices have been used. Are they, of them-

[51] Sangmeister, *Force and Fear as Precluding Matrimonial Consent*, p. 147.

[52] Cappello, *De matrimonio*, I, n. 465.

[53] De Smet (+ 1927), *Tractatus theologico-canonicus de sponsalibus et matrimonio* (ed. 4, Brugis: Beyaert, 1927), n. 646; Aertnys-Damen, *Theologia moralis*, II, n. 732; Cappello, *De matrimonio*, I, n. 462; Leitner (+ 1929), *Lehrbuch des katholischen Eherechts* (3. Aufl., Paderborn: Schöningh, 1920), p. 102.

[54] E.g., Grandclaude (+ 1883), *Ius canonicum* (3 vols., Parisiis, 1882-1883), III, 43, note 1. Cf. Esmein-Génestal-Dauvillier, *Le mariage en droit canonique*, II, 283.

selves, sufficient to constitute a moral violence which gives rise to the impediment of abduction? It is difficult to determine what answer the modern canonists give to this question. Several of them state that flattery, etc., can be the equivalent of moral violence, but it is not easy to exclude the possibility that this may mean that through them fear or fraud may be caused.[55] Augustine[56] and Knecht[57] mention respectively flattery and allurement as being sufficient to give rise to the impediment, but it is quite probable that they too have in mind the allurement and flattery which is used to deceive the woman.[58]

In France, however, it was maintained that this impediment existed also in the case of abduction through subornation or seduction, although here too there is much importance attributed, especially by the canonists, to the element of fraud which was frequently presumed.[59] This institute, however, never formed part of the universal law of the Church, nor was it ever legitimately a canonical impediment. It was, in fact, enforced in France through royal ordinances which claimed the right to regulate the French Church practice.[60]

It does not seem possible to admit that these devices could in any case constitute that moral violence which is required for giving rise to this impediment. While it is true that through them the passions of the woman might be provoked and thus the freedom of her act diminished, so that her subjection to the

55 E.g., Payen, *De matrimonio*, I, n. 1269; Gasparri, *De matrimonio*, I, n. 658; Schiappoli, *Il matrimonio secondo il diritto canonico e la legilazione concordataria italiana* (Napoli: Alvano, 1932), pp. 174-175.

56 *Marriage Laws and Matrimonial Trials*, p. 194.

57 *Handbuch*, p. 445.

58 Köstler says that flattery is almost unanimously considered to suffice for begetting the violence requisite in effecting the impediment. However he cites for this view Leitner, Wernz-Vidal, Triebs, and Cappello — all of whom speak only of fraud or intrigue as being enough. Cf. *Das oesterreichische Konkordats-Eherecht*, p. 61, note 2.

59 Cf. Mitterer, "Der Rapt de seduction als Ehehindernis nach gallikanischem Kirchenrecht." — *Zeitschrift der Savigny-Stiftung für Rechtsgeschichte, Kanonistische Abteilung*, XII (1922), 55-109.

60 Cf. Mitterer, *art. cit.*, and *Geschichte*, p. 116.

power of the man might come about at a time when she was not fully master of her will, it does not seem that this would be enough to effect the impediment. In fact, unless the woman is detained by the man through physical or moral violence in the true sense, i.e., by the inflicting of fear, she does not suffer any effectual restriction of her liberty in marriage. She can, when the passions have subsided and she is again capable of a truly deliberate act, free herself from that power. If the passions do not subside until after the marriage has taken place, the marriage will be adjudged according to the general principles on consent. If there was sufficient deliberation of the will to effect a true marital consent, then there is no doubt that the marriage was valid.

There remains, of course, always a possibility that these devices might be used as a means of inflicting grave fear, particularly if the man who abducts the woman has some species of superiority or of dominance over the woman. In such a case. there would certainly be an impediment of abduction. It is perhaps only the practical difficulty which would be experienced in proving such a species of fear that draws many authors to exclude absolutely the *raptus seductionis* from the impediment of abduction or detention.[61]

B. *The Finality of the Violence Employed.*

The violence which is used by the abductor or detainer must be directed towards placing the woman in the man's power. Only in that way can there be any question of the impediment of abduction or violent detention. This is the common doctrine of the canonists, although there is a slight inaccuracy in the manner of its expression. It is customary to state that the violence may be directed either towards the abduction and the marriage, or towards the abduction alone, or towards the marriage alone.[62]

61 Merkelbach, *Summa theologiae moralis,* III, n. 895; Vlaming (+ 1935), *Praelectiones iuris matrimonii ad normam Codicis Iuris Canonici* (3. ed., 2 vols., Bussum in Hollandia, 1919-1921), I, n. 310.

62 Wernz-Vidal, *Ius matrimoniale,* n. 311; De Smet, *De sponsalibus et*

This is correct inasmuch as in the last instance they contemplate the case in which intrigue is used as a means of obtaining influence over the woman. However, it is not to be understood as meaning that moral violence would be sufficient to give rise to the invalidity of the marriage even without some accompanying violence in the act of abduction or of detention. Hence it is perhaps preferable to state simply that the violence must be present in the act of abduction or detention which is perpetrated with a view to the contracting of marriage. The forceful act of which the man is the author must be one which places the woman effectively under the man's power for the purpose of marriage.

The woman must be, therefore, abducted unwillingly: she must be unwilling to be abducted for the purpose of marriage. It is of course immaterial whether her unwillingness in this act is directly concerned with the abduction alone or with the marriage alone. Thus she may desire marriage with the man, but object to the method (i.e., the abduction or detention) employed by him to attain his desire of marrying her. In such a case the impediment certainly exists. On the other hand, she may be entirely willing to be abducted, but be unaware of his intention, and be unwilling to be abducted for marriage. In such a case the impediment will not come into existence until she is first detained by means of moral violence employed by the man, i.e., it will exist from the moment that the woman is unwillingly held by the man for the purpose of marriage. It is obvious that, when the woman objects both to the abduction and to the intended marriage, the impediment is present in its most perfect form.

The violence which is used against the woman must therefore be directed precisely towards the abduction for the purpose of marriage. It must be present in the very first moment in which she comes into the power of the man. It must be employed to force her into the power of the man for the purpose of marriage. Even if the woman were for some other reason in the power of the man, there must be violence in her detention. The impedi-

matrimonio, n. 646; Schönsteiner, *Grundriss des kirchlichen Eherechts,* p. 364.

ment will then arise from the moment in which she is first detained for the purpose of marriage.

The only case which may cause some difficulty is that rare one in which the woman is fully aware that the man is abducting her with the intention of marrying her, and yet she permits this for some reason of her own, while at the same time she rejects the idea of marriage. Usually this will occur when the woman desires, for some personal reason, e.g., that of avoiding parental supervision, to escape from her home. She feels that once this desire is actualized she will be able to avoid marrying the man. In this case it does not seem that the impediment exists.[63]

Although the woman is rendered less free, this has happened as a result of her own free act, and there has been no real violence at all. Indeed, from the viewpoint of the Church's law regarding matrimonial impediments, there has not even been a canonically formal abduction, since her coming into the power of the man proceeds as much from her own volition as from any action on the man's part. Ordinarily, however, the physical act of abduction may be followed by some detention of the woman on the man's part. This detention may very easily come to be of a violent character, thereby giving rise to the impediment in its other form: violent detention. If force is used not to detain the woman, but merely to obtain her consent to the marriage, the impediment of abduction or violent detention will not be present, but rather it will be necessary to refer to the prescriptions of canon 1087 on defective consent.

The violence necessary for giving rise to the impediment of abduction must be of such a kind that the use of it contemplates the abduction with a view to contracting marriage. It must be formally directed towards this purpose, at least partially, else the impediment will not exist. A woman is violently abducted or detained as long as she objects to having her freedom to marry diminished through the violent act by which she comes into the power of the man.

63 Mitterer, *Geschichte*, pp. 113-115.

C. The Person Who Is Forced.

According to the almost unanimous opinion of the canonists who have written since the Code of Canon Law was published, the violence which gives rise to the impediment of abduction must be used against the woman abducted. It is not sufficient that such violence be used against the parents or guardians.[64]

The contrary opinion, which was solidly probable before the Code, seems to have been completely abandoned by modern canonists. It is somewhat difficult to assign a reason for this, since this opinion had some foundation in the pre-Code law. The better opinion, however, for some time has certainly been that which denied the presence of the impediment when violence was used against the parents. This opinion, in fact, corresponds better to the purposes of the law both of the Council of Trent and of the Code. The intention of the Council was to protect the freedom of the consent of the person involved, a freedom which was in no way jeopardized by the parent's objection. The law of the Code looks to exactly the same purpose which motivated the Tridentine legislation. Consequently the interpretation which harmonizes the import of the law of the Code with that of the Council of Trent appears to be the preferable interpretation of the current Code law.

The present writer, however, would hesitate in denying some speculative probability to the opinion which asserts the continued retention in the law of the impediment of *raptus in parentes*. The pre-Code decisions of the Congregation of the Council and the continued division of canonists down through the period following the Council of Trent seem to demonstrate the presence of a real doubt of law as to the meaning of the

64 Thus, e.g., Cappello, *De matrimonio*, I, n. 462; Schönsteiner, *Grundriss des kirchlichen Eherechts*, p. 364; Triebs, *Praktisches Handbuch*, p. 353; Chelodi (+ 1922), *Ius matrimoniale iuxta Codicem iuris canonici* (ed. 3, Tridenti: Tridentum, 1921), n. 90.

Gross (+ 1906)-Schueller (*Lehrbuch des katholischen Kirchenrechts*, 8. Aufl., Wien: Manzsche, 1922, p. 267) state that the canonical practice of the Church still recognizes the impediment when the woman is abducted against the will or without the knowledge of the parents.

decree of the Council. There does not seem to be anything in the Code of Canon Law to obviate that doubt. The fact that the Code employs the generic word *mulierem* and the fact also that the Code does not expressly except girls of minor age from its prescription in canon 1074 are hardly cogent reasons for asserting that the Code desired to resolve a very ancient and very celebrated controversy.[65] Certainly, to achieve that effect a clearer expression of the legislator's will was to be expected.

Even when one admits that the continued binding force of such an impediment is speculatively probable, nevertheless all practical force must be denied to the contention that this impediment still exists in the law because of the principle of canon 15. A doubtful impediment is, in effect, no impediment at all.[66] It is consequently licit to conclude, as almost all of the modern canonists do, that the impediment of abduction or of violent detention will exist only in the case wherein some violence has been used against the woman herself.

Article III — The Necessary Intention

The Code of Canon Law clearly states that, if the impediment is to arise, then the abductor must carry off the woman for the purpose of contracting marriage with her.[67] The same requirement with relation to the purpose of the perpetrated act is explicitly made when there is question of the impediment of violent retention.[68] If a woman is taken away, therefore, for any purpose other than that of marriage, e.g., for the purpose of extortion or of turpitude, the impediment does not arise. The marriage contracted between the abductor and his victim will be valid provided that the woman freely consents and that no other obstacle or impediment stands in the way.

Although the Council of Trent did not clearly express its mind on this point, the Sacred Congregation of the Council

65 These reasons are adduced by Cappello, *De matrimonio*, I, n. 462.

66 De Smet, *De sponsalibus et matrimonio*, n. 648.

67 Canon 1074, § 1.

68 Canon 1074, § 3.

authentically interpreted the Council's decree in this sense in a declaration dated January 23, 1586.[69] Despite this decree and its subsequent confirmation in particular cases,[70] a few authors held that abduction for any purpose was sufficient to give rise to the impediment,[71] but their opinion was devoid of probability even before the promulgation of the Code.[72]

Furthermore the intention of the abductor must be that of abducting the woman for marriage with himself. A man who abducts a woman in order that he may thereby render possible or more convenient her marriage with a third party does not fall under the impediment. And if the third party in question was unaware of the abduction, and did not in any way consciously contribute to it, he is not precluded by the impediment of abduction from contracting a valid marriage with the abducted woman.[73] If the man for whom the woman is abducted is aware of the abduction and its purpose, and in any way takes part in the violent act, even if only by encouragement or by material assistance, he will become subject to the impediment. If, however, he holds himself passively, and does not cooperate with the actual abductors, even though he does not oppose their sinister designs, and, in fact, may rejoice in them, he does not contract the impediment.[74] In order that the impediment arise, the man must not only have the intention of marrying the woman; he must also, in some way, be penally responsible for the abduction or detention.[75] It is, of course, obvious that the

69 Gallemart (+ 1625), *Sacrosanctum oecumenicum Concilium Tridentinum*, in sess. XXIV, c. 6.

70 E.g., S. C. C., *Brugnaten.*, 14 nov. 1648 — cited by Riganti, *Commentaria in regulas, constitutiones, et ordinationes Cancellariae Apostolicae*, in reg. 49, n. 54.

71 E.g., Emmanuel Sa (+ 1596) — cited by Sanchez, *De sancto matrimonii sacramento*, lib. VII, disp. XIII, n. 3; Guttierez (fl. 1618), *Canonicae quaestiones, tr. de matrimonio*, c. 86, n. 21; Collet (+ 1770), *Traité des dispenses en general et en particulier* (3 vols., Louvain, 1760), I, 308.

72 Wernz, *Ius Decretalium*, IV, n. 280, note 34.

73 Gasparri, *De matrimonio*, I, n. 642; Cappello, *De matrimonio*, I, n. 467.

74 Payen, *De matrimonio*, I, n. 1296.

75 Canon 2209.

impediment will arise from the fact of violent retention if, after someone else has abducted the woman for him without his assistance, or even without his knowledge, the man with whom marriage is intended detains the woman forcibly. The impediment in this case will arise at the moment the woman is first forcibly detained by a man who desires thereby to obtain marriage with her.

It is not necessary for the verification of the impediment that the intention to marry be the only intention present or that it be an absolute intention. A dual intention, e.g., of extorting money and of marrying the woman, would suffice. Likewise, a conditional intention, e.g., if the money is not received, then marriage will be forced, is enough to give rise to the impediment. Such a conditional intention would also be present when a woman is abducted by an agent who intends marriage with her in the event that the person who has ordered the abduction finds it impossible to reduce his own intention of marriage to action.

The intention to marry must be present in the very beginning of the abduction or detention, i.e., at the time when the violence which gives rise to the impediment is placed.[76] It is not enough that such an intention should come into being after the woman has been detained for another reason. However, the first act of violent detention which occurred while this intention was in the mind of the abductor or detainer would give rise to the impediment.

This case was the subject of much discussion before the Code, especially if the woman had been abducted for immoral purposes and was afterwards forcibly detained for marriage. The greater weight of opinion was with those authors who affirmed the presence of the impediment in such a case,[77] but the contrary opinion was sustained by some prominent canonists.[78]

If a woman is abducted for immoral purposes and of her

[76] De Smet, *De sponsalibus et matrimonio,* nn. 649, 651.

[77] Among those who held this were Gasparri, *Tractatus canonicus de matrimonio* (Parisiis, 1892), I, n. 546; Mansella, *De impedimentis,* p. 18; Leurenius, *Forum ecclesiasticum,* lib. IV, tit. I, cap. IX, III, n. 5.

[78] E.g. Schmalzgrueber, *Ius ecclesiasticum,* lib. V, tit. XVII, n. 44.

own accord asks the abductor to marry rather than to violate her, there is no impediment. Similarly, if the man abducts her for such illicit purposes, and, after he has violated her, offers her marriage as a remedy, or yields to her request for such a remedy, there is no impediment, provided, of course, that the woman has never been violently detained for the purpose of marriage.[79]

The presence of the impediment seems doubtful if the woman is abducted or violently detained for a purpose other than that of marriage, and then, while still remaining under the power of the abductor, is no longer violently detained. This case is very similar to the controverted case of the old law, since there is an initial act which has no relation to the impediment, followed by a set of circumstances which are not explicitly covered in the law. The same reasons would, in fact, stand for the assertion of the impediment in this case as in the old law, namely, the obvious difficulty of proving the details of the abductor's intention and the necessity of safeguarding, even in such a case, the freedom of the woman who, while not any longer violently held, is nonetheless subject to the influence of her abductor. Impediments, however, are subject to a restrictive interpretation as regards both their scope and extent,[80] and consequently it seems juridically more tenable to deny the presence of the impediment in the case. Practically, of course, the doubt of law will, in any event, deprive the controverted impediment of binding force.[81]

It is the intention of contracting marriage which is required in order that this impediment come into existence. When the abduction is perpetrated for some other purpose, the liberty of the woman to marry is ordinarily not limited. Any limitation which does occur in this regard is rather an incidental result of the abduction, and consequently is not included within the scope of this impediment, but in its possible effect upon the validity of the marriage must be adjudged with reference to the general

79 Vermeersch-Creusen, *Epitome iuris canonici*, II, n. 350.

80 Canon 19.

81 Canon 15.

laws which safeguard the freedom of marriage.[82] It is not required, however, that the man have the intention of contracting a valid marriage, for, even if he knows that the woman is prevented from validly marrying him in view of some other diriment impediment, the impediment of abduction will arise, and correspondingly must be removed in some way before any marriage can be celebrated between the two, even though the other impediment may meanwhile have ceased to exist either by reason of an altered personal status or in consequence of a granted dispensation. It is enough that the man intended to have the woman as his wife in so far as that is possible. His knowledge that the marriage will be invalid does not necessarily exclude a real intention to marry, just as it does not exclude the concomitant possibility of exchanging a real matrimonial consent.[83]

It is more difficult to decide whether such an intention to marry would exist if the man intended to contract only a civil marriage. An absolute answer can hardly be given to this question. In countries such as the United States where, unfortunately, civil marriage is accepted, even by some Catholics, as an ordinary means of acquiring the married state, an abduction which would envision such a marriage would certainly bring into existence the impediment of abduction. In other countries, where the Catholic tradition and teaching have had a more potent influence, and where, consequently, civil marriage is relatively rare, it is somewhat more difficult to concede that if a man intended such a union, he really also had an intention of marriage, as distinguished from the intention of keeping a woman for sexual gratification.

Even in this case, however, the present writer is inclined to admit that the impediment of abduction is present, for the liberty of the woman to marry is effectively curtailed through such a civil marriage. The intention of the legislator in establishing the law on abduction consequently seems to require that this case be comprehended. Impediments, however, are of restrictive interpretation. Hence, whenever a doubt of law remains,

82 Cf. especially canon 1087.

83 Canon 1085.

the existence of the impediment may justly be denied in view of the rule of canon 15 which disclaims binding force for any law whose import is shrouded in doubt.

When the civil marriage is intended as a means whereby the man will more easily be enabled to gratify his passions, or possibly as a means of obtaining a more effective power over the woman, the intention to marry may or may not be present in the sense of canon 1074. It will be present if the man intends, by means of the civil marriage, to give the woman the status of a wife; if he has no such intention, the intent to marry—which intent is necessary if the impediment of abduction is to arise—will not be present.[84]

It is, of course, the actual intention which determines the man to the action which is here considered. If a man were repeatedly but falsely to state that he was abducting the woman for immoral purposes, all the while really intending to obtain thereby marriage with his victim, the impediment would certainly arise in the internal forum. However, as Payen notes, if the woman is forced to accept marriage in order to avoid violation, the marriage will probably be null because of force and fear.[85]

[84] The intent to marry would, for example, seem to be absent were a man, who has abducted a woman in order to reduce her to prostitution, then to marry her civilly the better to conceal his crime.

[85] Payen, *De matrimonio*, I, n. 1275, note 5.

CHAPTER V

THE SUBJECT AND OBJECT OF THE ABDUCTION OR DETENTION

The impediment of abduction or detention has its origin in a violent act of abduction or detention. It is customary to speak of the person who commits the violence as the subject of the abduction or detention, and of the person who suffers the violence as the object. There are certain questions which refer to these two persons under these particular aspects. These questions will be treated in the present chapter. Before any discussion of these special questions is undertaken, however, certain other matters which regard both parties in relation to the impediment insofar as they are subject to the law of the Church must be investigated.

First of all, since the impediment of abduction and detention, considered in itself, inasmuch as it does not involve the defect of consent which frequently accompanies it, is entirely of the ecclesiastical law; it binds only those who are subject to that law. Hence infidels are not bound by this impediment when they intermarry,[1] unless the same impediment existed in the civil law to the jurisdiction of which they are subject.[2]

When an unbaptized person abducts a baptized person, the impediment of abduction constitutes an obstacle to their marriage because of the subjection of the baptized party to the law

1 McCloskey, *The Subject of Ecclesiastical Law according to Canon 12*, The Catholic University of America Canon Law Studies, n. 165 (Washington, D. C.: The Catholic University of America Press, 1943), p. 100.

2 This is now considered the only tenable teaching on this point, although some pre-Code canonists taught the opposite. Cf. Gasparri, *De matrimonio*, I, nn. 240-241; Cappello, *De matrimonio*, I, nn. 75-79.

In the United States of America no civil jurisdiction considers abduction or detention as an impediment to marriage, although most States punish abduction as a crime. Cf. Alford, *Ius matrimoniale comparatum* (Roma: Anonima Libraria Cattolica Italiana, New York: P. J. Kenedy and Sons, 1938), p. 122, n. 178.

of the Church. The impediment in fact exists in order to protect the liberty of the abducted person.[3] If the abductor is a baptized person and the woman abducted is not baptized, marriage is still impossible,[4] because the impediment is intended not only as a protection for the abducted person, but also as a deterrent of the crime of abduction or detention.[5]

All baptized persons are subject to this impediment whether or not they are members of the Catholic Church.[6] Heretics and schismatics are therefore subject to this impediment in the same way as Catholics.

There has been some doubt regarding the Oriental schismatics. The better opinion is that they are not subject to the laws of the Latin Church, but to the laws of the Oriental Catholic Church which corresponds to their rite.[7] Oriental Catholics are not subject to the law of the Code but to their own laws. These laws, however, incorporate the impediment of abduction as a diriment impediment in the sense in which it was established by the Council of Trent.[8]

If a woman belonging to the Latin rite is abducted by a man of any Oriental rite (schismatic or Catholic), the impediment of abduction or detention will exist in the exact sense in which it is contained in the Code because of fact that the woman is

3 Chelodi, *Ius matrimoniale*, n. 89.

4 This was denied by Van de Burght (+ 1883), *Tractatus de dispensationibus matrimonialibus* (Sylvae-Ducis, 1865), n. 55.

5 Cf. *infra*, pp. 72-73. The impediment is not of course a penalty of the crime of abduction, but it is intended as a deterrent of that crime and consequently has some penal aspects.

6 Cf. McCloskey, *op. cit.*, pp. 135-136.

7 Herman, "Reguntturne Orientales dissidentes legibus matrimonialibus Ecclesiae latinae?" — *Periodica de re canonica, morali, liturigica* (Brugis et Romae, 1905-), XXVII (1938), 7-20. The contrary opinion was sustained by Dalpiaz, "An Orientales schismatici legibus matrimonialibus Ecclesiae latinae teneantur" — *Apollinaris* (Romae, 1928-), X (1937), 457-459, and Oesterle, "Noch einmal ein Russehe" — *Theologische-praktische Quartalschrift* (Linz, 1832-), XC (1937), 680-684. According to reliable authority the opinion of Herman is actually followed by the Sacred Congregation for the Oriental Churches.

8 Cappello, *De matrimonio*, II, n. 914.

subject to the law of canon 1074. The same will be true if the abductor is a member of the Latin rite, and the woman abducted belongs to an Oriental rite (schismatic or Catholic), since in this case the man is under the rule of canon 1074. If, however, both the abductor and his victim are members of the same or different Oriental rites, the impediment will be interpreted according to the law of the proper Oriental Catholic churches, and will ordinarily, therefore, be understood in the sense in which it was contained in the Council of Trent.

Article I — The Subject of the Abduction or Detention

The impediment of abduction or detention will arise only if the subject of the act of abduction or violent detention is a man. There is no impediment if a woman abducts a man. Marriage contracted after such an abduction between the woman and her victim would be valid unless some other impediment would be present, or the man's consent would be defective. The Code of Canon Law has authentically decided the controversies which existed in the old law by inserting the word *vir* in qualification of the abductor, and the word *mulier* in circumscription of the abducted person.

Before the Code this same doctrine had been for a long time the more probable opinion,[9] but there were solid arguments for the contrary opinion.[10]

The impediment arises whether the abductor acts personally or through agents.[11] Even if the entire affair is handled by agents, that is, if the woman is abducted by them, and detained by them up to the actual moment of the marriage, the impediment renders marriage impossible between the man who ordered

9 It was already called the more probable opinion by Fagnanus (+ 1678), *Commentaria in libros Decretalium* (5 vols., Romae, 1661), ad c. 5, X, *de constitutionibus*, I, 2 — n. 372.

10 De Iustis (fl. 1691), *De dispensationibus matrimonialibus*, lib. II, c. XVIII, n. 72. Cf. also Gasparri, *Tractatus canonicus de matrimonio* (1892), I, n. 544. While sustaining the more probable opinion, Gasparri did not deny the operative force of the arguments of the other opinion.

11 Reg. 72, R. J., in VI°; cf. also canon 2209, §3.

the abduction and the woman whom he ordered abducted. The agents themselves will not ordinarily be subject to the impediment, since they will rarely themselves have any intention of marrying the woman. If such an intent were present on their part, however, they would also be prevented from marrying the abducted woman.[12]

It is not necessary that the person who desires through the abduction or detention to obtain marriage with the woman be the principal agent in such an act. Thus the abduction may be ordered and effected by some other person, yet the impediment arises only between the woman, on the one hand, and the man for whom the woman is being abducted, on the other. In order to be subject to the impediment, the man must of course have taken some part in the abduction.[13] The imputability of any action which would render him at least in part penally responsible for the abduction or detention, in accord with the principles of canon 2209, is enough to cause the invalidity of a marriage contracted with the abducted woman while she remains in the power of her abductors.[14] Thus if, knowing the abduction and its purpose, he encourages those who actually perpetrate the act, or gives them some material assistance, e.g., by providing an automobile with which to accomplish the abduction, he will be prevented from marrying the woman concerned. In all these cases, of course, he must have the intention of placing the woman thereby in a condition in which his own marriage will be facilitated. When this intention exists, any active cooperation on his part with the actual perpetrators of the abduction or detention will make his marriage with the abducted woman impossible in view of the contracted impediment.

The actual abduction or detention may be performed by women as well as by men, provided that it is intended as a means to effect marriage for the involved man with the woman who is

12 Cf *supra*, pp. 58-59.

13 Cf., e.g., S. R. Rota (Vic. Ap. Mandchuriae Septentrionalis) *Nullitatis matrim.*, 6 iun. 1917, *coram R. P. D. Amadori — Acta Apostolicae Sedis* (Romae, 1909-), X (1918), 207-215. Hereafter cited *AAS*.

14 Triebs, *Praktisches Handbuch*, p. 354.

abducted.[15] It seems that the impediment would arise also if the parents of the woman detained her in her own home, provided that the man had in some way been responsible for their action.[16]

Article II — The Object of the Abduction or Detention

The object of the abduction or detention must always be a woman if the impediment of abduction is to come into question. The abduction of a man gives rise to no impediment.[17] The character of the woman is immaterial; the impediment arises even from the abduction or detention of a woman of loose morals. The attempt of some writers to introduce the Roman law prescription that women of loose morals could not be considered as the object of this impediment met with no success in the canonical forum.[18]

If the woman who is abducted is otherwise impeded from marriage with the man, the impediment will nonetheless arise if she has been abducted for the purpose of attempting marriage with her. Hence married women, close relatives of the abductors, and girls not yet of marriageable age may all be the objects of the violent act, and will be unable to marry validly with their abductor until the conditions of canon 1074, §2, are fulfilled.[19] In these cases the impediment of abduction or detention will exist along with the other impediment, and both must cease before marriage will be possible.

A special difficulty was encountered in the historical inter-

15 Cf. S. C. C., *Parisien.*, 27 aug. 1864 — *Analecta iuris pontificii,* VII (1864), 1108-1116; S. C. C., *Praemislien.*, 18 iul. 1778 — *Thesaurus,* XLVII, 168-173.

16 Augustine, *Marriage Laws and Matrimonial Trials*, p. 194.

17 Cf. *supra*, p. 65.

18 La Croix (+ 1714) *(Theologia moralis,* lib. III, pars II, n. 636) mentioned Beckmann (+ 1556) as supporting the view that the abduction of prostitutes did not give rise to the impediment.

19 Knecht (+ 1932), *Handbuch*, p. 444. The contrary opinion was held by Guttierez (+ 1618), *Canonicae quaestiones, tr. de matrimonio,* c. 86, n. 21.

pretation of the Tridentine legislation when there was question of the abduction of an engaged or betrothed woman. The Decretal law did not consider such an abduction as *raptus* at all. This principle, which had its origin in the older meaning of the word *sponsa,*[20] had not been changed despite the change in the meaning of the term. The law of the Council of Trent, although it was intended for safeguarding the liberty of the abducted person, adopted the definition of *raptus* as it stood in the older law. It was only natural, then, that some of the commentators should fail to realize the importance of the change in the purpose of the legislation on *raptus,*[21] and thus feel that even after the Council of Trent there could be no *raptus propriae sponsae.*[22]

The great majority of canonists, however, applied to this question the consideration of the freedom of marriage which the Council had especially safeguarded. Hence they freely admitted that there was no impediment of abduction if a man carried off his own betrothed with her consent. If she objected to the abduction and had some just reason for breaking the *sponsalia,* then she was certainly prevented from marrying her abductor by the impediment of abduction. If there was no such reason for dissolving the betrothals, a few authors taught that the impediment did not exist.[23] The greater number of the canonists saw in the violence which was used in the abduction a sufficiently grave reason for breaking the *sponsalia,* since the man had no right to force on his own private authority the fulfillment of the be-

[20] Originally *sponsa* indicated primarily the *sponsa de praesenti.* Cf. Esmein (+ 1913), *Le mariage en droit canonique,* I, 133-141.

[21] The Decretal law was primarily penal, whereas the Tridentine regulations on abduction intended principally the protection of the liberty of the abducted person. Cf. Fourneret, *Le mariage chrétien* (5. ed., Paris: Beauchesne, 1925), pp. 243-244.

[22] Among those who taught this are: Barbosa (+ 1649), *Collectanea doctorum, tam veterum quam recentiorum, in ius pontificium universum* (6 vols. in 5, Lugdini, 1716), lib. V, tit. XVII, cap. VI; Scherer (+ 1918), *Handbuch des Kirchenrechtes,* II, 381, note 23; Freisen (+ 1933), *Geschichte des canonischen Eherechts,* p. 612, note 59.

[23] E.g., Pichler (+ 1736), *Ius canonicum,* lib. IV, tit. I, n. 119; Pirhing (+ 1679), *Ius canonicum* (5 vols., Dilingae, 1674-1677), lib. V, tit. XVII, sect. I, IV, n. 28.

trothal contract. Hence in every case wherein a man abducted his own betrothed against her will, they asserted the presence of the impediment.[24]

Since the promulgation of the Code the opinion that the abduction of his own betrothed by the abductor certainly gives rise to the impediment has been universally accepted.[25]

Salsmans, however, states that it seems necessary to recur to the Holy See if the betrothed woman did not have any just reason for breaking the espousals, whenever there is question of declaring the nullity of the marriage.[26] In justification of this opinion he cites a declaration of the Sacred Congregation for the Propagation of the Faith.[27] This response of the Congregation refers explicitly to the crime of *raptus,* and not to the impediment; hence it cannot be said to render certain the opinion proposed by Salsman. Furthermore it antedates the Code, which has made important changes in the law on betrothals. In the law of the Code, in fact, the nature of the obligation arising from valid *sponsalia* has, according to canonists of very great authority, been changed completely. Wernz-Vidal, for example, assert that there does not arise from the espousals any obligation which is determined precisely for the sake of effecting marriage. The obligation is rather a conditional one, namely, either of contracting marriage or of making satisfaction for any damages which have resulted when the pact of the betrothal has been left unfulfilled.[28] Gasparri admits that an obligation to contract

24 E.g., Schmalzgrueber (+ 1735), *Ius ecclesiasticum universum,* lib. V, tit. XVII, n. 40; Sanchez (+ 1610), *De sancto matrimonii sacramento,* lib. VII, disp. XIII, n. 15; Feije (+ 1894), *De impedimentis,* p. 95; Bangen (+ 1865), *Instructio practica de sponsalibus et matrimonio* (4 vols. in 1, Monasterii, 1858-1860), II, 144-145.

25 E.g., Wernz-Vidal, *Ius matrimoniale,* n. 312; Gasparri (+ 1934), *De matrimonio,* I, n. 644; Cappello, *De matrimonio,* I, n. 466.

26 Genicot (+ 1900), *Institutiones theologiae moralis* (ed. 13 recognita a I. Salsmans, 2 vols., Bruxellis: Édition Universelle, 1936), II, n. 496.

27 S. C. de Prop. Fide, 17 apr. 1784 — *Collectanea S. Congregationis de Propaganda Fide* (Romae, 1893), n. 1418.

28 *Ius matrimoniale,* n. 96, note 81. The same opinion is sustained by Claeys Bouuaert-Simenon, *Manuale iuris canonici* (3 vols., vols. I et III, 3

marriage still arises, now as formerly, from the betrothal, but he maintains that this obligation has been changed from a grave obligation of justice to a light obligation of fidelity.[29] In both of these opinions, then, there is no right on the part of the man to exact marriage from the woman: hence she cannot be forced by abduction into such a marriage. The impediment of abduction will certainly arise from the abduction of the abductor's betrothed.

Even if the contrary and more common opinion is admitted, i.e., that the betrothal gives rise to a serious obligation, binding in justice, of marrying the betrothed person,[30] it must still be admitted that the impediment of abduction will arise from the abduction of the betrothed woman, for, if the man cannot force by the public authority of the ecclesiastical court the fulfillment of the promise of marriage,[31] he certainly may not do so by means of a violent abduction, i.e., on his own private authority.

There does not seem to be any reason, therefore, for doubting the certainty of the teaching of all the canonists that the impediment of abduction will arise even from the abduction of the abductor's bethrothed, provided that an act of real violence be committed in the abduction. Hence it is hardly necessary to refer such cases to the Holy See; the nullity of such a marriage could be declared by a diocesan court in the usual fashion.

ed., 1930; vol. II, 1931, Gandae et Leodii: Prostant apud auctores in Seminario Gandavensi et Leodiensi), II, 209-211.

29 *De matrimonio*, I, n. 99-103.

30 This opinion is sustained by the great majority of modern canonists, e.g., Cappello, *De matrimonio*, I, n. 107; Payen, *De matrimonio*, I, n. 274; Schönsteiner, *Grundriss des kirchlichen Eherechts*, p. 124; De Smet (+ 1927), *De sponsalibus et matrimonio*, p. 17.

31 Canon 1017, §3.

CHAPTER VI

THE NATURE, CHARACTER, DURATION AND CESSATION OF THE IMPEDIMENT

Article I — The Nature and Character of the Impediment

The impediment of abduction and detention, if it be considered abstractly, belongs entirely to the ecclesiastical law. In relation to marriage, it establishes a hindrance that is dependent on a set of circumstances which, in divine law, in no way affects the validity of the marriage. In a concrete case wherein the impediment of abduction is verified, however, the impediment of abduction will usually be accompanied with an obstacle which probably derives nullifying force from the natural law, namely, with a defective consent because of the presence of force and fear. The violence which is present in every case wherein the impediment occurs is, in fact, very apt to cause such fear. Indeed the act of violence has such fear as its almost connatural result. Consequently most marriages which are invalid on account of the impediment of abduction or detention could also be attacked because of the presence of defective consent. Both reasons for nullity ordinarily exist together.

A careful distinction must be drawn between the elements of force and fear, which invalidate the marriage because of a defective consent, and the impediment of abduction and detention, which renders the marriage null because of a hindrance enacted by ecclesiastical authority. In the first place force and fear will give rise to the impediment of abduction or detention if they are present at the beginning of the abduction or detention, even though they have ceased before the actual exchange of consent. On the other hand, a marriage will be null on account of *vis et metus* only if the consent is defective at the moment it is exchanged. Moreover, the impediment of abduction depends on certain definite circumstances to which the effect of incapacitating the persons for marriage is attached by the ecclesiastical law, whereas the elements of force and fear prescind from all circumstances, and consider only the character of the consent expressed, namely, whether or not it is actually free. If the consent is defective, the marriage is invalid probably by reason of the natural law alone.[1] Finally the purposes of the two institutes only partially coincide; both are established to protect the freedom of matrimonial consent, but the impediment of abduction safeguards only that of the woman, while the invalidity arising from force and fear defends equally the man and the woman from external influences. The impediment of abduction is moreover intended as a deterrent of the crime of abduction.

The impediment of abduction establishes a legal incompetence affecting both parties and rendering them incapable of exchanging a valid matrimonial consent. It is not, therefore, in any sense a presumption *iuris et de iure* of non-consent, as a few authors have less accurately called it.[2] The impediment invalidates the marriage of its own force, independently of any presumed lack of consent.

A general presumption of non-consent whenever a woman has been abducted was one of the principal motives which led the legislator to introduce the impediment. This presumption, however, is not a juridical presumption in the technical sense, but rather a general fear and suspicion of non-consent in such a case.[3]

The principal purpose of the impediment is, therefore, the protection of the woman's freedom in contracting marriage, which protection aims to render secure the element of liberty and the consideration of the dignity of Christian marriage.[4] The impediment is consequently not primarily penal in character, al-

1 It is at least solidly probable that force and fear invalidate be reason of the natural law alone. The contrary opinion is also probable. Cf. Sangmeister, *Force and Fear as Precluding Matrimonial Consent*, pp. 154-163.

2 Santi (+ 1885)-Leitner (+ 1929), *Praelectiones iuris canonici*, lib. IV, tit. I, n. 153; De Angelis (+ 1881), *Praelectiones iuris canonici* (4 tom. in 8 vols., Romae-Parisiis, 1877-1884. Tom. IV ed. N. Gentili), lib. IV, tit. I, n. 20. Cf. Gasparri, (+ 1934), *De matrimonio*, I, n. 638; Wernz (+ 1914), *Ius Decretalium*, IV, n. 275, note 3.

3 Cappello, *De matrimonio*, I, n. 471.

4 Sipos, *Enchiridion iuris canonici* (3 ed., Pécs: Haladás, 1936), p. 577.

though it has a penal aspect. In fact, the criminal act in which it has its origin is deprived of its intended effect through this impediment, and this is done, naturally, not only because of the necessity of safeguarding the freedom of the woman, but also on account of the horror and indignation of the legislator at such a crime.[5] The incompetence to marry which is thus established has a penal aspect inasmuch as it effectively prevents the abductor from obtaining the desired marriage through his criminal act. This penal character is subordinate, however, to the primary intent of the law, for, as soon as the woman's freedom has been established in the manner prescribed in canon 1074, § 2, the impediment ceases, even though the man may not yet have repented of his crime nor have made any satisfaction.[6]

The impediment of abduction or detention is a relative impediment, that is, it renders the abductor and the abducted woman incapable of marriage with each other as long as she remains in the man's power. It is not a hindrance, however, to the marriage either of the man or of the woman with any other person. Such a marriage, even if contracted by the woman while she is still under the influence of her abductor, would not be affected by this impediment.

The impediment is diriment in character, but this point hardly need be labored. The invalidating effect is abundantly clear in the text of canon 1074, § 1: *"inter virum raptorem et mulierem . . . raptam . . . nullum potest consistere matrimonium."*

Article II — The Duration and Cessation of the Impediment

The impediment of abduction or detention ceases not only through legitimate dispensation but also by the operation of the law itself on the verification of the conditions specified in canon

[5] Cf. S. C. S. Off., instr. (ad Ep. Albaniae, 15 febr. 1901 — *Fontes*, n. 1250).

[6] The ecclesiastical penalties for the crime, which are established in canon 2353, are not, of course, taken away when the impediment ceases. Cf. Triebs, *Praktisches Handbuch*, p. 237.

1074. In the present article this automatic cessation will first be treated, then cessation through dispensation. Finally a few remarks will be added on the requirements for cessation in the case of the simple convalidation or radical sanation of a marriage when it has been attempted in contravention of the prescriptions of canon 1074.

A. *Cessation by Operation of Law*

The term of duration for the impediment of abduction and detention is indicated in the light of two rules contained in canon 1074. In canon 1074, § 1, the impediment is said to exist "*quandiu ipsa in potestate raptoris manserit.*" In canon 1074, § 2, the cessation of the impediment is explicitly treated:

> **Quod si rapta, a raptore separata et in loco tuto ac libero constituta, illum in virum habere consenserit, impedimentum cessat.**

In the latter quoted section, the legislator has determined a particular set of circumstances under which the impediment ceases, while in the earlier section he has established the impediment for only that period during which the woman remains in the power of the man.

The first problem which arises in connection with this automatic cessation of the impediment is, consequently, the concordant interpretation of these two texts. There are two possible interpretations. In the first place, the legislator may have laid down a general principle in canon 1074, § 1, and then in canon 1074, § 2, have authentically stated one case in which such a condition would be verified. Or, on the other hand, the two texts may be precisely equivalent: the woman is in the power of her abductor, at least in a juridical sense, until the conditions of canon 1074, § 2, are fulfilled.

This latter interpretation must certainly be accepted, for it is absurd to suppose that the legislator would set up definite conditions for the cessation of the impediment, and then, in the same immediate context, allow cessation even without the verification of these conditions. The *potestas raptoris*, therefore, which is mentioned in canon 1074, § 1, is primarily a juridical status, which exists as long as the conditions of canon 1074, § 2, are not actually fulfilled.

This interpretation seems to be commonly accepted by modern canonists,[7] but some authors speak less accurately — in a way, in fact, which seems to reflect an interpretation similar to the first one proposed above. Thus, for example, Cappello says that the woman is not free from the abductor's influence, at least by a contrary presumption, until the conditions of canon 1074, § 2, have been fulfilled.[8] Such a presumption would allow proof to the contrary, and consequently it would be possible to have a case wherein the impediment ceased, even though one or the other of the conditions had not been verified.[9] The same impression is given by a number of authors who omit explicit mention of the conditions, either entirely or in part, and thereby imply that these are not absolute requirements of the law.[10]

There is really only one requirement in canon 1074, § 2: that the woman shall have consented to marriage with the abductor after she has been separated from him and placed in a free and safe place. The emphasis of the law seems to be placed, therefore, on the consent of the woman, but two conditions are postulated under which that consent must be given. These conditions are required absolutely; unless they are verified, the impediment does not cease, and there can be no valid marriage between the abductor and his victim, even if she

7 Cf. Gasparri, *De matrimonio,* I, n. 650; Payen, *De matrimonio,* I, n. 1285.

8 *De matrimonio,* I, n. 469. Cf., however, n. 474, where the other interpretation is very briefly expressed.

9 This would not be true, of course, if the presumption in question were an invincible presumption *(iuris et de iure).* A presumption of this type, however, is neither clearly stated in the canon, nor required for the proper interpretation.

10 E.g., Augustine (+ 1943), *Marriage Laws and Matrimonial Trials,* p. 195: "Freedom of consent is all that is required, and the impediment is removed as soon as this freedom is restored." Other examples: De Becker (+ 1936), *De matrimonio praelectiones canonicae* (ed. nova ad tramites C. I. C., Louvain: Ceuterick, 1931), p. 61; Farrugia, *De matrimonio et causis matrimonialibus,* p. 326.

freely and willingly consents to marry him.[11] They cannot be supplied in any way, not even by a solemn oath.[12]

The whole purpose of the law seems to require that the consent which is here mentioned be given while the woman is actually separated from the man, and resides in a free and safe place. The canon itself could, of course, be interpreted as demanding simply that the separation and placing of the woman in a free and safe place should precede the positing of the consent. Since the law is intended to establish certainty as to the woman's freedom, however, it seems better to require that this consent be given while the woman is actually separated from the abductor. If she has rejoined the man before the consent is given, it will be just as difficult to establish her freedom as if she had never left him.

The consent of which there is question is not the actual exchange of marital rights. The canon should rather be understood as indicating any consent to marriage, that is, even a promise of marriage in the future. The importance of this distinction lies in the fact that, if actual marital consent be required, the woman must remain separated from the abductor until the marriage ceremony takes place. If, on the other hand, the consent is understood as any promise to marry, then this is not necessary. Once the woman has given consent to a marriage with him while she is separated from him and in a free and safe place, the impediment has ceased, and if she rejoins him, there will not be any obstacle to their valid marriage, unless there has been a new act of violence.[13]

The two ideas — a free and safe place, and separation from the abductor — are very closely connected. In fact, they seem almost to coincide in some ways. Yet they are separate requirements of law, and consequently must both be verified before the impediment will cease. Nevertheless they are to be considered together and their final purpose is to be kept constantly in

11 Gasparri, *De matrimonio,* I, n. 650.

12 S. C. S. Off., instr. (ad Ep. Albaniae), 15 febr., 1901 — *Fontes,* n. 1250.

13 Cf. S. C. C., Ruben., 3 mart. 1714 — *Fontes,* n. 3131.

mind for any decision whether or not, in a given case, they are actually present. Through them the legislator seeks to assure the absence of every influence of the man over the woman. As a negative norm, then, it can be said with certainty that the conditions of law for the cessation of the impediment are never fulfilled when the woman is still under the influence of the abductor. The positive requirement is more difficult to determine.

a. *Separation from the Abductor.* The first requirement is that the woman be separated from her abductor. This entails, first of all, a physical[14] separation from the man himself and from his agents.[15] This regards especially the dwelling place; the woman must no longer be living in the same dwelling with the man.[16] The length of time for which this separation must endure is not established in the law. A few days are certainly sufficient if the woman enjoys perfect freedom and peace during that time.[17] No change of place on the part of the woman is absolutely required.[18] If the woman has been detained by the man, the separation will be effected by the departure of the man, provided, of course, that this place thereby becomes free and safe for the woman. The geographical distance between the abductor's dwelling and the place in which the woman is put away from him is, of course, of no particular import, as long as his influence has ceased.

b. *A Safe and Free Place.* A safe and free place is one in which the woman is able freely to dispose her affairs as she will, and in which she can declare her own wishes without external constraint.[19] A public place is not necessarily a free place, nor

14 Triebs, *Praktisches Handbuch*, p. 356.

15 S. C. S. Off., instr. (ad Ep. Albaniae), 15 febr. 1901 — *Fontes*, n. 1250; S. C. C. *Herbipolen.*, 24 apr. 1858; 18 iun. 1859 — *Fontes*, nn. 4162, 4176.

16 Payen, *De matrimonio*, I, n. 1285.

17 S. C. C., Ruben., 3 mart., 1714 — *Fontes*, n. 3131.

18 Triebs *(loc. cit.)* requires that the woman revert from the place of her detention to a free, safe, and secure place.

19 Cf. the remarks of the Secretary in S. C. C., *Olomucen.*, 29 iul. 1769 — *Thesaurus*, XXXIX (1769), 79.

is a place free for the simple reason that the woman is able to place some free acts there.[20]

A place can be said to be free and safe in this connection only if it is one in which the woman is entirely exempt from every influence of the abductor, whether this influence be exercised by him personally, by his agents, or by the external circumstances in which the woman has been placed. Thus, e.g., a very young woman can hardly be said to be in a free and safe place if the abductor deserts her in the midst of a large and strange city far from her home. The strangeness of the place and the confusion which it will engender in the woman's mind are, as it were, a continuation of the abductor's influence, for the woman will naturally conceive of them as proceeding from the man's evil act in placing her in such a condition.

The woman's own home, however, will usually be a safe and free place, provided that every influence of the man has been eliminated. Similarly the house of a friend or relative of the woman is considered safe and free, if the friend or relative has not favored the marriage with the abductor. Last of all, a monastery or similar house of refuge will ordinarily be free from the influence of the man in the necessary way.

Many modern canonists still require that the pastor consult the Ordinary before he assists at a marriage in which the impediment of abduction was present but later was removed in conformity with the rule of canon 1074, § 2.[21] In this they follow the opinion of several pre-Code canonists, who, however, based this opinion on the necessity of the bishop's intervention to establish the dowry which the abductor, by Tridentine law, was obliged to pay to the woman.[22]

20 S. C. C., *Parisien.*, 27 aug. 1864 — *ASS*, I (1865-1866), 21.

21 E.g., Gasparri, *De matrimonio*, I, n. 659; Cappello, *De matrimonio*, I, n. 474; De Smet, *De sponsalibus et matrimonio*, n. 650, note 2; Triebs, *Praktisches Handbuch*, p. 356.

22 De Iustis (fl. 1691), *De dispensationibus matrimonialibus*, lib. II, c. XVIII, n. 16; Pyrrhus (+ 1686), *Praxis dispensationum apostolicarum*, lib. VII, c. 66, n. 66; Feije (+ 1894), *De impedimentis*, p. 115.

Bangen (*Instructio practica de sponsalibus et matrimonio*, II, 145) required it because of the practical difficulty of deciding whether or not the conditions were fulfilled.

In the system of the present Code of Canon Law this consultation of the Ordinary is not necessary, unless there is some doubt as to the fulfillment of the conditions for the cessation of the impediment.[23] The pastor, in fact, has the duty of investigation whether or not there is a canonical impediment standing in the way of the celebration of the marriage.[24] If there is no such impediment and the other requirements of law have been fulfilled, then he is to admit the parties to the celebration of marriage.[25] If he doubts whether the impediment has ceased, then he must continue his investigations,[26] and only if the doubt still remains must he consult the Ordinary.[27] The bishop could, of course, reserve the right to judge in these circumstances to himself.[28] If certainty about the cessation of the impediment is difficult to obtain, then there appears at hand a sufficient reason for the bishop to issue a temporary prohibition of intermarriage to the parties in accord with canon 1039.[29]

In cases wherein there has been violent abduction (as distinguished from violent detention), the Ordinary's intervention will eventually be required to dispense the vindictive penalty which the abductor has incurred, namely, his exclusion from exercising in the Church acts specifically accredited in ecclesiastical law *(actus legitimi ecclesiastici)* and to impose the other penalties enjoined in canon 2353. This intervention of the Ordinary is not, however, required before the pastor assists at the marriage, since the *latae sententiae* penalty imposed in canon 2353 does not impede the reception of the sacraments.[30] In the case of violent detention such intervention of the Ordinary would not be at all necessary unless the abductor had used real physical

23 Thus, Payen, *De matrimonio*, I, n. 1285; Wernz-Vidal, *Ius matrimoniale*, n. 313, note 27; Schönsteiner, *Grundriss des kirchlichen Eherechts*, p. 368; Knecht, *Handbuch*, p. 448.

24 Canon 1020, § 1.

25 Canon 1031, § 3.

26 Canon 1031, § 1, 1°.

27 Canon 1031, § 1, 3°.

28 Canon 1020, § 3.

29 Knecht, *Handbuch*, p. 448.

30 Canon 2256, § 2.

violence in the abduction, and had been legitimately condemned, either in the civil or ecclesiastical forum, for his delict.[31]

B. *Cessation by Dispensation*

Since the impediment of abduction or detention is an impediment of the ecclesiastical law, the Church can dispense it. There are, however, usually connected with this impediment some elements of force and fear from which, since they probably invalidate marriage by the demand of the natural law itself, the Church does not dispense.[32] Consequently there can be no dispensation until the cessation of force and fear, if it be present, is assured, and the free consent of the woman has been made apparent. When this has been done, dispensation is possible.

Even in this case the Church only very rarely dispenses. The reason for this is obvious. The legislation of the Church provides a means whereby the impediment can be made to cease. Hence there will very rarely be any necessity for a dispensation. In an exceptional case circumstances may exist which may make such a dispensation necessary, namely, if the conditions established in canon 1074, § 2, cannot be fulfilled. In such a case, for very grave causes, the Church will dispense.[33]

There is a natural presumption that the woman's consent is not free as long as it is given while she is in the power of her abductor. This presumption must be overcome before any dispensation can be granted.[34] Hence, before a dispensation from this impediment may be granted, the following conditions must obtain: (a) absence of all force and fear which could affect the woman's consent; (b) certain proof of the freedom of the woman's consent; (c) grave inconvenience preventing the fulfillment of the conditions demanded in canon 1074, § 2, for the cessation of the impediment; (d) a very grave cause.[35]

31 Canon 2354. Cf. Vermeersch-Creusen, *Epitome iuris canonici*, III, n. 556.

32 Cf. *supra*, pp. 71-72.

33 S. C. S. Off., instr. (ad Ep. Albaniae), 15 febr. 1901—*Fontes*, n. 1250.

34 Gasparri, *De matrimonio*, I, n. 660.

35 Gasparri, *De matrimonio*, I, n. 661; Capello, *De matrimonio*, I, n. 474; Schönsteiner, *Grundriss des kirchlichen Eherechts*, p. 373.

In the pre-Code law the dispensation from this impediment was usually reserved to the Holy See itself,[36] but the faculty to dispense was sometimes given.[37] Dispensations granted by the Apostolic Datary from other marriage impediments contained the clause *dummodo mulier propter hoc rapta non fuerit.* This clause expressed a true condition and affected the validity of the dispensation. Hence, if the woman had been abducted, even though the impediment of abduction had ceased in accordance with the law, the dispensation granted by the Datary was invalid. It was consequently necessary to express the fact of abduction in the petition for all dispensations requested from Rome.[38]

In general faculties to dispense from impediments other than *raptus,* this condition was expressed in another form: *dummodo mulier propter hoc rapta non fuerit, et, si rapta fuerit, in raptoris potestate non existat.* In using these faculties the Ordinary had to attend only to the fact whether or not the woman actually was in the power of the man. If she was, the Ordinary could not dispense, and if, as a matter of fact, he did dispense, the dispensation was invalid.[39]

In the present law the impediment of abduction or detention is dispensed in ordinary circumstances only by the Holy See itself or in virtue of faculties conceded by it. Canons 1043-1045 contain a general faculty by means of which Ordinaries, pastors, and confessors are empowered, under certain conditions, to dispense from the impediments of abduction or detention when there is danger of death or when everything is in readiness for the wedding. It will be necessary for the bishop or priest when dispensing to comply not only with the special requirements of

[36] S. C. S. Off., instr. (ad Ep. Albaniae), 15 febr. 1901—*Fontes,* n. 1250.

[37] S. C. de Prop. Fide (C. P. pro Sin.—Sutchuen.), 31 ian. 1796—*Fontes,* n. 4647.

[38] S. C. C., 1 dec. 1583; 6 apr. 1606—Riganti, *Commentaria in regulas, constitutiones et ordinationes Cancellariae Apostolicae,* in Reg. 49, nn. 96-97; cf. Feije, *De impedimentis,* p. 116.

[39] S. C. de Prop. Fide (C. P. pro Sin.—Cochinchin.), 11 febr. 1804; 22 nov. 1860—*Fontes,* nn. 4679, 4851; S. C. de Prop. Fide, litt. (ad Ep. Natcheten.), 26 ian. 1877—*Fontes,* n. 4889; S. C. S. Off. (S. Ludovici), 15 iun. 1875—*Fontes,* n. 1042.

canons 1043-1045, but to assure himself also of the presence of the circumstances which are demanded for every dispensation from this particular impediment.[40]

It is doubtful whether the bishop can dispense from the impediment of abduction or detention when the impediment is only doubtfully present because some fact in the case is doubtful. Canon 15 grants the faculty to dispense from all ecclesiastical laws in which the Roman Pontiff is wont to dispense whenever there is a doubt of fact. Vromant holds that the Roman Pontiff is now accustomed to dispense from all matrimonial impediments of ecclesiastical law except the impediments arising from the sacred priesthood and the impediment of affinity in the direct line when the marriage has been consummated.[41] He deduces his argument from the very ample faculties (excepting only these two impediments) which the Holy See is accustomed now to grant for habitual use to Apostolic Nuncios and Delegates,[42] and to the Ordinaries of mission countries.[43]

This opinion, while it is opposed to the common teaching,[44] may be considered as probable and will therefore provide a safe norm for action in practical cases.[45] Hence the Ordinary, when

40 Cappello, *De matrimonio,* I, n. 474; Triebs, *Praktisches Handbuch,* p. 357.

41 Vromant, *Ius missionariorum,* tom. V, *De matrimonio* (Louvain: Museum Lessianum, 1931), nn. 92-94.

42 Cf. *Index facultatum Nuntiorum Apostolicorum,* n. 30 — Vermeersch-Creusen, *Epitome iuris canonici,* I, 637.

43 *Formula facultatum S. C. de Prop. Fide. Formula tertia (major),* n. *21 — Vermeersch-Creusen, *op. cit.,* I, 643. This faculty also excepts the impediment which arises from the defect of the required age for marriage.

44 E.g., Cappello, *De matrimonio,* I, n. 224; De Smet, *De sponsalibus et matrimonio,* n. 714 and p. 613, note 2; Payen, *De matrimonio,* I, n. 635. All of these authors include *raptus* among the impediments from which the Church is not accustomed to dispense.

45 Payen, *De matrimonio,* I, p. 475, note 3. Payen, however, limits his conclusion to Ordinaries of mission countries.

It is hard to see what practical utility the opinion would have in mission countries, since the Ordinaries of missions already have the power to dispense from all impediments (except nonage and the two mentioned above) by delegation from the Holy See.

the impediment is doubtful because the facts are doubtful, may dispense from the impediment. For the same reason it is probable that the Ordinary may also use canon 81 in relation to the impediment of abduction, when there is grave danger in delay and recourse to the Holy See is impossible. Almost the same requirement, in fact, is made in this canon as in canon 15, namely, that there be question of a dispensation which the Church is accustomed to give.

The Quinquennial Faculties of the bishops in the United States contain no faculty whereby they may dispense from this impediment, except that they are given authority, in certain cases, to grant a radical sanation when the marriage was contracted invalidly.[46] It has already been mentioned that Ordinaries in mission countries receive from the Sacred Congregation for the Propagation of the Faith faculties which enable them to dispense from this impediment.

The clauses which were formerly inserted in all dispensations concerning *raptus* are no longer used by the Holy See.[47] Hence it is not now necessary to mention the fact of *raptus* if another dispensation is asked, provided, of course, that the impediment of abduction has ceased and is not at present an obstacle to the marriage.[48]

C. *Simple Convalidation and Radical Sanation*

Since the impediment of abduction or detention arises from a violent act, it will ordinarily be susceptible of proof in the external forum. Hence it is usually a public impediment.[49] As a rule, therefore, a marriage which is invalid because of this impediment can be convalidated in the simple form only after

46 *Quinquennial Faculties of Ordinaries in the United States*—Bouscaren, *The Canon Law Digest* (2 vols., Milwaukee: Bruce, 1934-1943), II, 30-42.

47 Gasparri, *De matrimonio*, I, nn. 345, 662; Wernz-Vidal, *Ius matrimoniale*, n. 315; Vlaming, *Praelectiones iuris matrimonii*, n. 480.

48 Several authors still require that this be mentioned. Cf., e.g., Pruemmer, *Manuale theologiae moralis*, III, n. 821.

49 Canon 1037. Cf. *infra*, p. 89.

(a) the impediment has ceased, either through the operation of the law, or in consequence of a legitimate dispensation; and (b) the consent has been renewed in the prescribed legal form, i.e., before the proper priest and two witnesses.[60]

It may happen, however, that the violent act upon which this impediment is based will occur under circumstances in which the juridical proof of the impediment will be impossible. For example, the woman may be carried off secretly through the use of some drug. In such a case the impediment will be occult, and consequently may be convalidated by the secret renewal of the consent of the parties, exchanged in private, and without the intervention of the ecclesiastical authorities.[61]

A radical sanation can also be granted by the Holy See for marriages invalid because of abduction, as long as there is full proof of the freedom of the woman's consent in the marriage. There will naturally be very great practical difficulties in obtaining such certain proof in cases in which sanation provides the only remedy.

Nevertheless the Ordinaries of the United States, by virtue of their Quinquennial Faculties,[62] are able to grant such a sanation, even in the case of an impediment of abduction or detention, provided that one of the parties does not know of the nullity of the marriage, and that the renewal of consent cannot be obtained from this party without serious inconvenience. It is impossible, of course, that one of the parties to a violent abduction or detention should be ignorant of the fact of abduction or detention. But ignorance of the invalidating effect attached by law to this fact of abduction or detention is quite possible, and suffices for the use of this faculty.

60 Canon 1135, § 1.

61 Canon 1135, § 2.

62 *Quinquennial Faculties of Ordinaries in the United States,* Faculties of the Sacred Congregation of the Sacraments, n. 4—Bouscaren, *The Canon Law Digest,* II, 34.

CHAPTER VII

THE PROCEDURE IN CASES OF NULLITY OF MARRIAGE ARISING FROM THE IMPEDIMENT OF ABDUCTION OR DETENTION

A complete treatment, even in summary outline, of the procedure to be followed in the declaration of nullity of a marriage which has been invalidly contracted because of the presence of an impediment of abduction or detention is hardly necessary for the purposes of this dissertation. The present chapter, then, will treat only of those points in which the laws of procedure receive a special application in regard to the impediment of abduction or detention.

Canon 1990 contains an exhaustive list of the cases in which the summary process may be used to declare the nullity of a marriage.[1] Since this list does not contain mention of the impediment of abduction or detention, the declaration of nullity on account of this impediment will consequently require the observance of all the formalities prescribed in the law for the solemn judicial process.

Two points of this procedure require special attention in cases in which the impediment of abduction or detention is alleged: the right to impugn the validity of the marriage, and the proof of the existence of the impediment.

Article I — The Right to Impugn the Validity of the Marriage

The abductor is not capable of impugning the validity of the marriage which he has contracted after having abducted or violently detained his spouse, for he is the culpable cause of the impediment, and thereby also of the invalidity of the marriage.[2]

1 Cf. *Letter of Apostolic Delegate on Handling of Marriage Cases in the United States*, 23 Sept., 1938 — Bouscaren, *The Canon Law Digest*, II, 531.

2 Canon 1970, § 1, 1°. Cf. *Pontificia Commissio ad Codicis canones*

The abducted woman always has the right of impugning the validity of the marriage, because she is never the direct cause of the impediment. While it is true that she may have known of the impending nullity of the marriage to be contracted and may even have deceitfully concealed that fact before the marriage, even in that case she is not deprived of the right to impugn the marriage,[3] because she is neither the direct cause of the impediment, nor the direct cause of the nullity. The woman can never be the cause of the impediment of abduction, because this impediment must come into existence through an abduction or detention which is against her will. Consequently, she is never barred from denouncing in court the invalidity of her marriage as deriving from this impediment. If there are alleged for the nullity of the marriage other reasons of which she was the culpable cause, she may not be permitted to impugn the marriage unless she limits her case to the grounds of abduction alone.[4]

Contrariwise, the abductor can never be admitted as plaintiff in a marriage trial in which nullity is alleged in view of the impediment of abduction. Since he always places the act from which the impediment arises, and since this action is by supposition culpable, he must by necessary consequence be considered the culpable cause of the impediment.[5]

authentice interpretandos, 17 iul. 1933 (*AAS*, XXV [1933], 345); 27 iul. 1942 (*AAS*, XXXIV [1942], 241).

Cf. also Reh, "Guilt of the Plaintiff in a Marriage Case"—*The Jurist* (Washington, D. C., 1940-), III (1943), 404-415.

3 Canon 1970, § 1, 1°. Cf. Reh, *art. cit.*, p. 411; Gasparri, *De matrimonio*, II, n. 1260. The contrary opinion is presented by Doheny, *Canonical Procedure in Matrimonial Cases: Formal Judicial Procedure* (Milwaukee: Bruce, 1938), pp. 88-89.

4 Cf. *Interpretation of Instruction on Matrimonial Procedure* (S. C. de Sacr., 18 ian. 1938), n. 1—Bouscaren, *The Canon Law Digest*, II, 545.

5 Cf. Roberti, "Quando coniux dicendus sit dubie habilis ad accusandum matrimonium"—*Apollinaris*, XII (1939), 267-270.

The exact meaning of the expression *causa culpabilis impedimenti* has been the subject of much discussion. The statements in the text are based on the opinion which is called by Roberti in the article cited *longe probabilior*.

According to another view, the abductor could be admitted as plaintiff,

The right of the abducted woman to impugn the validity of her marriage should be used as soon as she has regained her liberty. The *Instructio Austriaca* enjoined that a woman who had not used this right immediately should no longer be heard.[6] This limitation has not been repeated in the present Code,[7] and the woman may at any time contest the marriage.[8] If, however, the woman delays for a considerable time without any apparent reason, the judge must inquire into the reasons for the delay. It will also, of course, be necessary to ascertain that the marriage has not been convalidated during the period of the delay.

If the abducted woman did not contest the marriage during the first six months after she had been restored to liberty, and lived in peaceful cohabitation with the abductor, there was, according to Wanenmacher, an inevitable presumption in the old law that the marriage had been convalidated by mutual consent. This presumption, of course, affected only those places in which the Tridentine law on the form of marriage was not in effect.[9] It does not seem to the present writer that such a presumption was ever established for the impediment of abduction. Wanenmacher cites articles 116 and 120 of the *Instructio Austriaca* and n. 36 of the Instruction of the Sacred Congregation for the Propagation of the Faith sent to the bishops of the United States in 1883.[10] Both of these documents speak only of *vis et metus* in the articles indicated, and the deduction that the same rules applied to *raptus* does not seem justifiable.

In any case, all such presumptions have been taken away by

if he did not know or intend the nullity of the marriage at the time he contracted it. This view is now denied all probability by Roberti, although in an earlier article he had sustained it. Cf. *Apollinaris*, VI (1933), 443.

6 N. 120 — *Collectio Lacensis*, V, 1302.

7 Schönsteiner, *Grundriss des kirchlichen Eherechts*, p. 372. Wernz-Vidal *(Ius matrimoniale*, n. 316) transcribe art. 120 of the *Instructio Austriaca*, and seem to imply that it still has some force of law.

8 Canon 1701. Cf. canon 1972.

9 Wanenmacher, *Canonical Evidence in Marriage Cases* (Philadelphia: Dolphin Press, 1935), n. 433.

10 *Instructio Austriaca*, art. 116, 120 — *Collectio Lacensis*, V, 1302; S. C. de Prop. Fide, instr. a. 1883, 36 — *Fontes*, n. 4901.

the present Code of Canon Law, which requires that the juridical form of marriage be observed in the entire Latin Church. Consequently, if the impediment from which the nullity of a marriage derives is public, such a marriage can be convalidated only through a renewal of consent in the solemn form. If the impediment is occult, convalidation is permitted secretly and privately without the observance of the laws regarding the form required for the contracting of marriage. In such a case, there might still be room for a presumption such as that mentioned by Wanenmacher. It would, however, be a personal presumption of the judge, and not a legal presumption.

The diocesan promoter of justice is also empowered by canon 1971, § 1, 2°, to impugn the validity of marriages when there is question of an impediment which is *natura sua publicum*. The exact meaning of this phrase has been the subject of considerable controversy since the very promulgation of the Code.[11] The Roman Rota, in a decision dated August 11, 1928, interpreted this phrase in the sense of the known pre-Code distinction between the impediments of public interest *(iuris publici)* and those of private interest *(iuris privati)*. The former are those which have been instituted principally for the public good and for the protection of the public respect and sanctity of marriage. Impediments of private interest are those which are established principally, but not exclusively, for the good of the private individuals concerned.[12] This interpretation seems to be the more favored one at present and is certainly a safe norm in practice.[13]

[11] Cf., e.g., Hilling, "Studien zum Eherecht des Codex Juris Canonici: I. Die öffentlichen und geheimen Ehehindernisse" — *AKKR*, CII (1922), 1-17; Köstler, "Was sind 'öffentliche Ehehindernisse'?" — *AKKR*, CXVI (1936), 57-87; Glynn, *The Promoter of Justice* (The Catholic University of America Canon Law Studies, n. 101, Washington, D. C.: The Catholic University of America, 1936), pp. 152-168.

[12] S. R. Rota (Augustodunen.) *Nullitatis matrim.*, 11 aug. 1928, *coram R. P. D. Wynen* — *S. R. Rotae decisiones seu sententiae* (Romae, Typis Vaticanis, 1912-), XX (1928), 402-412.

[13] Cf. Hilling, "Das Klagerecht bei Eheprozessen und die Römische Rota" — *AKKR*, CXVI (1936), 442-445.

In this sense the impediment of abduction or detention is certainly an impediment of public interest as long as the woman remains in the power of the man. A few authors are of the opinion that once she has been released from the man's power this impediment becomes one of private interest, and that therefore the promoter of justice cannot impugn the validity of such a marriage.[14] This limitation is not mentioned by other canonists.[15]

This distinction between the time preceding the separation of the parties and the time following limits considerably the right of the promoter of justice. There seems to be no reason for admitting such a limitation only in the case of abduction. The marriage contracted by the woman while in the power of the man remains null even after she has been released from that power, just as any other marriage contracted invalidly remains invalid after the two individuals concerned have separated. On the other hand, the marriage will continue to be considered as juridically valid in the eyes of the ecclesiastical authorities until some declaration of the presence of the impediment of abduction has been made, even though the parties have separated. Nor is it necessary to conclude that only the private good of the parties will be served by a declaration of nullity when the parties are no longer cohabiting. The very juridical recognition of a marriage which is the result of a violent act might easily be the cause of scandal for the removal of which the action of the promoter of justice might be required.

Hence it may be concluded that the promoter of justice is empowered to impugn the validity of any marriage which is invalid because of the impediment of abduction, even after the woman has been released from the power of her abductor.[16]

14 Schönsteiner, *Grundriss des kirchlichen Eherechts,* p. 372; Wernz-Vidal, *Ius matrimoniale,* n. 316; Knecht, *Handbuch,* p. 450.

Schönsteiner, however, notes that this opinion (which he calls universal) has no foundation in the law.

15 Linneborn (+1933), *Grundriss des Eherechts nach dem Codex Iuris Canonici* (2-3 Aufl., Paderborn: Schöningh, 1922).

16 The same conclusion can be admitted even if the interpretation of *natura sua publicum,* as given above, is denied. Even though understanding

The abductor himself and any other person who knows of the invalidity of the marriage may denounce this to the Ordinary or to the promoter of justice. The promoter of justice, however, may not act on the denunciation of the abductor unless the following circumstances are present: (a) the impediment is capable of proof in the external forum, and its existence is not open to serious doubt; (b) the public good, i.e., the removal of scandal, demands the accusation of the marriage; (c) the marriage, despite the cessation of the impediment, cannot now be celebrated validly.[17] If the abductor is a non-Catholic, the promoter of justice moreover cannot impugn the validity of the marriage unless, in the prudent judgment of the Ordinary, the public good demands it.[18]

Article II — The Proof of the Existence of the Impediment

In order to prove the presence of the impediment of abduction or detention, each of the three elements which go to make up the impediment must be conclusively shown. Thus it will be necessary to demonstrate (a) that there was actually either an abduction or a detention of the woman by the man; (b) that that detention or abduction was accompanied by violence; (c) that the man had at the time of the abduction or detention an intent to marry. The impediment is not proved as long as any one of these facts remains in doubt. It will also be necessary to show that the marriage was never convalidated after the impediment had ceased.

The unanimous teaching of the canonists is that the fact of the abduction or detention must be incontrovertibly proved. It

this phrase as meaning an impediment which arises from a fact which of its nature is capable of proof in the external forum, some authors list *raptus* as an impediment public of its very nature. Cf., e.g., Santoro, "Le facoltà per le dispense matrimoniali dell'Ordinario, del parroco . . ." — *Il monitore ecclesiastico* (Maratea-Conversano-Roma, 1876-), XXXIX (1927), 333.

17 S. C. de Sacr., instr., 15 aug. 1936, art. 39 — *AAS*, XXVIII (1936), 322. Cf. Bouscaren, *The Canon Law Digest*, II, 482.

18 S. C. S. Off., 22 mart. 1939 — *AAS*, XXXI (1939), 131; Bouscaren, *The Canon Law Digest*, II, 547.

is never to be presumed.[19] Once this fact is proved, however, there are, according to almost all the canonists who wrote both before and since the Code, several presumptions which aid in determining the presence of the remaining elements of the impediment of abduction. The reason for asserting these presumptions is obvious. Both the intention of the man and the violence used against the woman are factors which are capable of determination only by means of an investigation into the mind and the will of the parties. Such an investigation is never without its difficulties, and the presumptions established are of the utmost practical value.

The principal presumptions that are established are the following:

I. *In regard to the purpose of marriage.*

Whenever a woman has been abducted, and has been joined in marriage with the abductor while she remained in his power, it is to be presumed that the man abducted her for the purpose of marriage. This presumption exists even though he has not previously approached the girl or her parents with the intention of asking for her hand in marriage, but it is much stronger if some such attempt to obtain her for himself has occurred.[20] If the woman who is abducted is not respectable, but is, e.g., a prostitute, she is presumed to have been willingly abducted for immoral purposes and not for marriage.[21]

II. *In regard to the violence used.*

If the woman consented to the abduction, it is always presumed that she was induced to give her consent through some kind of violence. Hence the presumption generally stands against

19 Riganti (+ 1735), *Commentaria in regulas, constitutiones et ordinationes Cancellariae Apostolicae,* in Reg. 49, n. 62; Wanenmacher, *Canonical Evidence in Marriage Cases,* n. 518.

20 *Instructio Austriaca,* n. 173 — *Collectio Lacensis,* V, 1310; Gasparri (+ 1934), *De matrimonio,* I, n. 461; Payen, *De matrimonio,* I, n. 1271; Chelodi (+ 1922), *Ius matrimoniale,* n. 104; Wanenmacher, *Canonical Evidence in Marriage Cases,* n. 518.

21 Cappello, *De matrimonio,* I, n. 466; Gasparri, *De matrimonio,* I, n. 643; Payen, *op. cit.,* I, n. 1270.

the abductor. If, however, the man had made some approaches to the girl before the abduction concerning marriage, then there is no longer a presumption of violence. On the other hand, if the woman abducted is a girl of minor age, and her parents are unaware of, or opposed to, the abduction, the presumption of violence is much greater.[22]

If the woman did consent to the abduction, but the abduction is proved to have been for some other purpose than marriage, then any matrimonial consent given by the woman while she remained in the power of her abductor is presumed to have been forced.[23]

Before the present Code of Canon Law these presumptions were considered to be presumptions of law, and most of the present-day canonists seem to continue to regard them as such even after the Code.[24]

There seem to be grave difficulties in such an opinion. Canon 1014 asserts the presumption which governs all matrimonial procedure: in doubt the marriage is always to be presumed valid until the contrary is proved. Now these presumptions which are asserted in the case of abduction directly contradict this norm of canon 1014. In fact, they presume the existence of a diriment impediment, and therefore the invalidity of the marriage. Hence they can hardly any longer be sustained as presumptions of law, particularly since they are nowhere expressed in the new law.[25]

22 Chelodi, *Ius matrimoniale*, n. 104; Wernz (+ 1914)-Vidal (+ 1938), *Ius matrimoniale*, n. 314; Knecht (+ 1932), *Handbuch*, p. 446; Gasparri, *De matrimonio*, n. 641; Vermeersch (+ 1936), *Theologia moralis*, III, n. 725; Wanenmacher, *Canonical Evidence in Marriage Cases*, n. 518.

23 *Instructio Austriaca*, n. 173 — Collectio Lacensis, V, n. 1310; Wanenmacher, *op. cit.*, n. 518.

24 Cf. Cappello, *De matrimonio*, I, n. 468; Gasparri, *De matrimonio*, I, n. 641, note 1.

Wanenmacher *(Canonical Evidence in Marriage Cases*, nn. 387, 518-519) seems to consider them in the same light, although in another place (n. 392) he says that these presumptions which are not explicitly repeated in the new law are "legal in a wider and secondary sense, and they are sometimes called factual presumptions."

25 As a matter of fact they were never authentically stated in the old

Wanenmacher cites canon 2200, §2, and asserts that when the fact of abduction along with the subsequent marriage has been proved, the elements of the impediment which lie hidden in the will of the parties are to be presumed by a rebuttable presumption.[26] This application of canon 2200, §2, can hardly be admitted. The canon states: "When an external violation of the law has taken place, *dolus* is always to be presumed in the external forum." *Dolus* is defined as the deliberate will to violate the law (canon 2200, §1). It is hard to see what connection this deliberate will to break the law has with the purpose of marriage or the presence of violence. The canon presumes that the abductor deliberately broke the law of the Church. It does not presume that he broke it in the definite way in which the impediment of abduction comes into existence.

Furthermore, canon 2200, §2, finds its proper application in penal matters; it is a penal canon and consequently cannot properly be extended to non-penal matters. On the basis of this canon a presumption may be made to the effect that the man who abducted a woman did so deliberately, and therefore incurred the penalties for abduction as listed in canon 2353. The crime of abduction and the impediment are not, however, the same; the impediment sometimes exists without the crime, and vice versa. Consequently, the presumption will not apply to all cases of abduction. It seems extremely doubtful, too, that this canon can be applied to the presumption of the hidden elements even of the crime of abduction. The crime is not even externally committed until the woman is abducted either for the purpose of marriage or for an immoral purpose. The intent of the man is a necessary constituent of the violation of the law itself; if it is not present, there is no crime. Hence the presumption of canon 2200, §2, does not apply until the intent either of contracting marriage or of indulging concupiscence is proved.

It appears necessary, therefore, to consider these presumptions as personal presumptions *(praesumptiones hominis)*, that is, as

law, but were introduced through doctrinal interpretation and especially through canonical jurisprudence.

[26] *Canonical Evidence in Marriage Cases*, n. 518.

conjectures based on the usual course of events which the judge will invoke when the determined facts given above are present in the case.[27] Understood in this sense, they will be of the very greatest utility, for they will frequently assist in solving practical doubts which remain even after continued investigation.

As personal presumptions, however, they will not constitute full proof, especially not the proof which would be required for the declaration of the nullity of a marriage. On the other hand, the presumption of law is a full proof.[28] To overthrow such a legal presumption the contrary must be fully proved. Hence a personal presumption by itself can never be sufficient to prevail against the legal presumption of canon 1014. The presence of the impediment of abduction can never be asserted on the basis of the presumptions given above without some additional proof.[29]

The investigations of the judge may, however, fail to establish conclusively the fact of violence or the presence of the purpose of marriage, while at the same time he uncovers a number of indications and partial proof to that effect. In such a case the personal presumptions which have been outlined above may assist in the formulation of moral certitude as to the presence of the fact in question. In other words, these personal presumptions of the intent of marriage and of violence, while not of themselves sufficient to overthrow the legal presumption for the validity of the marriage, may, in conjunction with other proofs, engender moral certainty of the presence of the impediment.

The above related presumptions will, moreover, be extremely useful to the pastor in the pre-nuptial investigation of a mar-

27 Schönsteiner (*Grundriss des kirchlichen Eherechts*, p. 366) states this explicitly in regard to the purpose of marriage. Cf. also Gougnard, *Tractatus de matrimonio* (ed. 7a ad normam Codicis recognita, Mechlinae: Dessain, 1937), pp. 414-415.

28 Cf. Manning, *Presumption of Law in Matrimonial Procedure* (The Catholic University of America Canon Law Studies, n. 94, Washington, D. C.: Catholic University of America, 1935), p. 16.

29 Cf. Rerum Scriptor, "Incipit lamentatio Vinculi . . ."—*Apollinaris*, XII (1939), 381. The author establishes the principle: *"Contra iuris praesumptionem praesumptio hominis vix admittitur,"* but is perhaps too stringent in its application.

riage in which he suspects the presence of an act of abduction or detention. In such circumstances these presumptions, properly modified, may be used to settle the doubts. The pastor will be justified in enjoining on the parties a separation, etc., in accordance with canon 1074, §2, with a view that the impediment, if present, may certainly be removed.[30]

30 Gougnard, *Tractatus de matrimonio*, pp. 414-415.

CONCLUSIONS

1. The violence which is necessary for giving rise to the impediment may be either a physical or a moral violence, provided only that the woman be actually unwilling in the abduction or detention. Such moral violence is not present unless the woman has been coerced by means of real fear.

2. The violence necessary for this impediment must be of such a kind that the use of it contemplates abduction with a view to marriage. It must be formally directed towards that purpose, at least in part.

3. Violence against the parents is not enough; it must be directed against the woman herself. The contrary opinion, even if it be admitted as speculatively probable, has no practical force in the present law of the Church.

4. The abductor must have at least a partial or conditional intention of abducting the woman for marriage with himself at the time he places the violent act of abduction or detention from which the impediment arises. The impediment will arise between the woman and any man who had this intention and was penally responsible in any way for the abduction or detention.

5. The intention of contracting a valid marriage is not required; it is enough that the man intend thereby to give the woman the status of a wife, at least in the common estimation.

6. The abductor must be a man, but he may act either personally or through agents, regardless of whether the accomplices be men or women.

7. The abduction of any woman, even of the betrothed of the abductor, effects the impediment.

8. Abduction inasmuch as it is an impediment is strictly of the ecclesiastical law. Its purpose is to protect the freedom of the woman in contracting marriage. It is not a penalty for the crime of abduction, but it does have some penal aspects.

9. The impediment ceases only when the woman is released from the power of the abductor. The *potestas raptoris* is a juridical state which exists until the woman is separated from

the abductor, is placed in a free and safe place, and has indicated her willingness for marriage with the man. Separation from the abductor must be both a physical and a moral separation. A free and safe place is one in which the woman is entirely beyond the reach of any influence employable by the man, whether that be exercisable by him personally, or through agents, or through the external circumstances in which she has been placed.

10. The pastor is competent to declare the cessation of the impediment even without consulting the ordinary, provided that there is no doubt as to the fulfillment of the conditions required in canon 1074, §2.

11. Dispensation from the impediment of abduction in ordinary cases is reserved to the Holy See, but faculties to dispense are sometimes given. Such faculties are contained for extraordinary cases in canons 1043-1045. It is doubtful that the bishop can dispense in virtue of the norms enacted in canons 15 and 81.

12. If the marriage is invalid because of the impediment of abduction alone, the abducted woman is always competent to impugn the validity; the abductor can never do so. The promoter of justice can impugn the validity even after the woman has been released from the power of her abductor.

13. The presumptions which were used in the pre-Code jurisprudence for establishing the existence of the impediment can no longer be considered as legal presumptions. They may serve, however, as personal presumptions of the judge, but do not constitute full proof of the presence of the impediment.

BIBLIOGRAPHY

Sources

Acta Apostolicae Sedis, Commentarium officiale, Romae, 1909- .

Acta et decreta sacrorum conciliorum recentiorum. Collectio Lacensis, 7 vols., Friburgi Brisgoviae: Herder, 1870-1890.

Acta Sanctae Sedis, 41 vols., Romae, 1865-1908.

Bouscaren, T. Lincoln, *The Canon Law Digest,* 2 vols., Milwaukee: Bruce, 1934-1943.

Codex iuris canonici Pii X Pontificis Maximi iussu digestus Benedicti Papae XV auctoritate promulgatus, Romae: Typis Polyglottis Vaticanis, 1934.

Codicis iuris canonici fontes cura Emi Petri Card. Gasparri editi, 9 vols., Romae (later Civitate Vaticana): Typis Polyglottis Vaticanis, 1923-1939. (Vols. VII, VIII, IX, ed. *cura et studio Emi Iustiniani Card. Seredi.)*

Collectanea S. Congregationis de Propaganda Fide, Romae, 1893.

Concilium Tridentinum, Diariorum, Actorum, Epistularum, Tractatuum nova collectio, edidit Societas Goerresiana, 13 vols. (incomplete), Friburgi Brisgoviae, 1901- .

Corpus iuris canonici, ed. Lipsiensis secunda, post Aemilii Ludovici Richteri curas instruxit Aemilius Friedberg, 2 vols., Lipsiae, 1879-1881.

Corpus iuris civilis, 3 vols., Berolini, 1928-1929. (Vols. I - II, P. Krueger ed.; Vol. III, R. Schoell - G. Kroll ed.)

Decretales D. Gregorii Papae IX, una cum glossis restitutae, Romae, 1582.

Decretum Gratiani emendatum et notationibus una cum glossis illustratum, Venetiis, 1605.

Gallemart, Ioannes, *Sacrosanctum et oecumenicum Concilium Tridentinum, additis declarationibus Cardinalium Concilii interpretum, ex ultima recognitione Ioannis Gallemart, nunc demum hac postrema editione adnotationibus D. Card. de Luca illustratum,* Tridentini, 1737.

Jaffé, Phillipus, *Regesta Pontificum Romanorum ab condita Ecclesia ad annum post Christum natum MCXCVIII,* 2 ed. (Kaltenbrunner, Ewald, Loewenfeld), 2 vols., Lipsiae, 1885-1888.

Krueger, P., *Codex Theodosianus,* Berolini: apud Weidmannos, 1923-1926.

Mansi, J. D., *Sacrorum conciliorum nova et amplissima collectio,* 53 vols. in 59, Paris-Leipzig-Arnhem, 1901-1927.

Monumenta Germaniae historica, 188 vols. (incomplete), Hannoverae, 1826-;
Leges, tom. II, ed. G. H. Pertz, 1837;
Leges in 4°, Sectio II, *Capitularia Regum Francorum,* tom. I, ed. A. Boretius, 1883;
Sectio III, *Concilia,* tom I: *Concilia aevi merovingici,* ed. F. Maasen, 1893.

Pallottini, Salvator, *Collectio omnium conclusionum et resolutionum quae in causis propositis apud Sacram Congregationem Cardinalium S. Concilii*

Tridentini Interpretum prodierunt ab eius institutione anno MDLXIV ad annum MDCCCLX, 17 vols., Romae, 1868-1893.

Potthast, Aug., *Regesta Pontificum Romanorum*, 2 vol., Berolini, 1874-1875.

S. R. Rotae decisiones recentiores, 19 parts in 25 vols., Francofurti-Aureliae-Romae, 1623-1703.

S. R. Rotae decisiones seu sententiae, Romae: Typis Polyglottis Vaticanis, 1912- .

Thesaurus resolutionum Sacrae Congregationis Concilii, 167 vols., Romae, 1718-1908.

Authors

Aegidius Bellamerae, *Commentaria in Gratiani Decretum*, Lugduni, 1550.

Aertnys, J. - Damen, C. A., *Theologia moralis*, 13a ed., 2 vols., Taurini-Romae: Marietti, 1939.

Alford, Culver Bernard, *Ius matrimoniale comparatum*, Romae: Anonima Libraria Cattolica Italiana — New York, P. J. Kenedy & Sons, 1938.

Alphonsus Maria de Ligorio, S., *Theologia moralis*, ed. nova cura et studio P. L. Gaudè, 4 vols., Romae: Typis Polyglottis Vaticanis, 1905-1912.

Ayrinhac, H. A., *Marriage Legislation in the New Code of Canon Law*, revised and enlarged by P. J. Lydon, New York: Benziger, 1940.

[Bachofen], Charles Augustine, *A Commentary on the New Code of Canon Law*. Vol. V: *Marriage Law and Matrimonial Trials*, 5th rev. ed., St. Louis-London: Herder, 1935.

Bangen, Ioannes Henricus, *Instructio practica de sponsalibus et matrimonio*, 4 vols. in 1, Monasterii, 1858-1860.

Barbosa, Augustinus, *Collectanea doctorum, tam veterum quam recentiorum, in ius pontificium universum*, 6 vols. in 5, Lugduni, 1716.

Bernardus Papiensis, *Summa Decretalium*, ed. Ern. Ad. T. Laspeyres, Ratisbonae, 1860.

Billuart, Charles-René, *Summa Sancti Thomae hodiernis academiarum moribus accomodata*, ed. nova, 8 vols., Parisiis-Romae-Bruxellis, 1880-1900.

Cappello, Felix M., *Tractatus canonico-moralis de sacramentis*. Vol. III: *De matrimonio*, 4 ed., 2 toms., Taurinorum Augustae: Marietti, 1939.

Carrière, Joseph, *De matrimonio*, 2 vols., Parisiis, 1837.

Chelodi, Ioannes, *Ius matrimoniale iuxta Codicem Iuris Canonici*, ed. 3a, Tridenti: Tridentum, 1921.

Claeys Bouuaert, F. - Simenon, G., *Manuale iuris canonici*, 3 vols., Vols. I et III, 1930-1931; Vol. II, 1931, Gandae et Leodii: Prostant apud auctores in Seminario Gandavensi et Leodiensi.

Collet, Pierre, *Traité des dispenses en general et en particulier*, 3 vols., Louvain, 1760.

D'Annibale, J., *Summula theologiae moralis*, 3 vols., Romae, 1897.

De Angelis, Philippus, *Praelectiones iuris canonici ad methodum Decretalium Gregorii IX exactae*, 4 tom. in 8 vols., Romae-Parisiis, 1877-1884. (Tom. IV ed. N. Gentili.)

De Becker, Iulius, *De matrimonio praelectiones canonicae*, editio nova ad tramites Codicis Iuris Canonici accomodata, Louvain: Ceuterick, 1931.

De Iustis, Vincentius, *De dispensationibus matrimonialibus tractatus*, Lucae, 1726.

De Luca, Ioannes Baptista, *Theatrum veritatis et iustitiae*, 16 vols., Coloniae Agrippinae, 1706.

De Smet, Al., *Tractatus theologico-canonicus de sponsalibus et matrimonio*, ed. 4a (inde a Codice altera), Brugis: Beyaert, 1927.

Doheny, William J., *Canonical Procedure in Matrimonial Cases*, Milwaukee: Bruce, 1938.

Esmein, A., *Le mariage en droit canonique*, deuxiemé edition mise a jour par R. Génestal et J. Dauvillier, 2 toms., Paris: Recueil Sirey, 1929-1935.

Fagnanus, Prosper, *Commentaria in libros Decretalium*, 5 vols., Romae, 1661.

Falco, Mario, *Corso di diritto ecclesiastico*, Padova: Milani, 1930.

Farrugia, Nicolaus, *De matrimonio et causis matrimonialibus*, Taurini-Romae: Marietti, 1924.

Feije, Henricus Ioannes, *De impedimentis et dispensationibus matrimonialibus*, Lovanii, 1874.

Ferraris, F. Lucius, *Bibliotheca canonica, iuridica, moralis, theologica, necnon ascetica, polemica, rubricistica, historica*, ed. novissima, 9 vols., Romae, 1885-1899.

Fourneret, Pierre, *Le mariage chrétien*, 5 ed., Paris: Beauchesne, 1925.

Freisen, Joseph, *Geschichte des canonischen Eherechts bis zum Verfall der Glossenlitteratur*, 2. Ausgabe, Paderborn, 1893.

Gasparri, Petrus, *Tractatus canonicus de matrimonio*, ed. altera, 2 vols., Paris, 1892.

——, *Tractatus canonicus de matrimonio*, ed. nova ad mentem Codicis I. C., 2 vols. in 1, Typis Polyglottis Vaticanis, 1932.

Genicot, Eduardus, *Institutiones theologiae moralis*, ed. 13a quam recognovit I. Salsmans, 2 vols., Bruxellis: Edition Universelle, 1936.

Glynn, John C., *The Promoter of Justice*, The Catholic University of America Canon Law Studies, n. 101, Washington, D. C.: The Catholic University of America, 1936.

Gougnard, A., *Tractatus de matrimonio*, ed. 7 ad normam Codicis recognita, Mechlinae: Dessain, 1937.

Gross, Karl - Schueller, Heinrich, *Lehrbuch des katholischen Kirchenrechts*, Wien, 1922.

Grandclaude, E., *Ius canonicum*, 3 vols., Parisiis, 1882-1883.

Guttierez, Ioannes, *Canonicae quaestiones*, 3 vols., Noribergae-Lugduni, 1647-1661.

Henricus de Segusia (Cardinalis Hostiensis), *Commentaria in quintum Decretalium librum*, Venetiis, 1581.

——, *Summa aurea*, Venetiis, 1570.

Ioannes ab Anania, *Praelectiones in Decretalium librum quintum*, Lugduni, 1546.

Ioannes Andreae, *Novella super quinto Decretalium*, Venetiis, 1504.

Knecht, August, *Handbuch des katholischen Eherechts*, Freiburg im Breisgau: Herder, 1928.

Köstler, Rudolf, *Das österreichische Konkordats-Eherecht*, Wien: Springer, 1937.

——, *Die väterliche Ehebewilligung*, Kirchenrechtliche Abhandlungen herausgegeben von Ulrich Stutz, 51 Heft, Stuttgart, 1908.

——, *Wörterbuch zum Codex Iuris Canonici*, München: Kösel-Pustet, 1927-1929.

La Croix, Claudius, *Theologia moralis*, 3 toms., Ravennae, 1761.

Leitner, Martin, *Lehrbuch des katholischen Eherechts*, 3. Aufl., Paderborn: Schöningh, 1920.

Leurenius, Petrus, *Forum ecclesiasticum*, 3 vols., Venetiis, 1729.

Lindsay, W. M., ed., *Isidori Hispalensis episcopi etymologiarum sive originum libri*, Scriptorum classicorum bibliotheca Oxoniensis, Oxonii, 1910.

Linneborn, Johannes, *Grundriss des Eherechts nach dem Codex Iuris Canonici*, 2. und 3. Aufl., Paderborn: Schöningh, 1922.

Manning, John J., *Presumption of Law in Matrimonial Procedure*, The Catholic University of America Canon Law Studies, n. 94, Washington, D. C.: The Catholic University of America, 1935.

Mansella, Iosephus, *De impedimentis matrimonium dirimentibus ac de processu iudiciali in causis matrimonialibus notiones et disceptationes canonicae*, Romae, 1881.

Matharan, M. M., *Casus de matrimonio*, Parisiis-Matriti, 1893.

McCloskey, Joseph, *The Subject of Ecclesiastical Law according to Canon 12*, The Catholic University of America Canon Law Studies, n. 165, Washington, D. C.: The Catholic University of America Press, 1943.

Merkelbach, Benedictus Henricus, *Summa theologiae moralis*, 3 vols., Vols. I et II, 3. ed., 1938; Vol. III, 2. ed., 1936, Parisiis: Desclée.

Migne, J. P., *Patrologiae cursus completus, series graeca*, 161 vols., Parisiis, 1856-1866.

——, *Patrologiae cursus completus, series latina*, 221 vols., Parisiis, 1844-1864.

Mitterer, Max, *Geschichte des Ehehindernisse der Entführung im kanonischen Recht seit Gratian*, Görres-Gesellschaft zur Pflege der Wissenschaft im katholischen Deutschland, Veröffentlichungen der Sektion fur Rechts- und Sozialwissenschaft, 43 Heft, Paderborn: Schöningh, 1924.

Mommsen, Th., *Le droit pénal romain*, tr. par J. Duquesne, 3 vols., Paris, 1907.

Muñiz, T., *Procedimentos ecclesiasticos*, 2 ed., 3 vols., Sevilla, 1926.

Müssener, Hermann, *Das katholische Eherecht in der Seelsorgspraxis*, 2. Aufl., Düsseldorf: Schwann, 1933.

Nau, Louis J., *Manual on the Marriage Laws of the Code of Canon Law*, 2nd ed., New York-Cincinnati: Pustet, 1934.

Navarrus (Martinus de Azpilcueta), *Consiliorum seu responsorum . . . tomi duo*, 2 vols., Venetiis, 1621.

Nicholaus de Tudeschis (Abbas Panormitanus), *Commentaria in quartum et quintum librum Decretalium*, Venetiis, 1588.

Pallavicino, Pietro Sforza, *Istoria del Concilio di Trento*, con annotazioni di Francescantonio Zaccaria, 6 vols., Faenza, 1792-1797.

Payen, G., *De matrimonio in missionibus ac potissimum in Sinis tractatus practicus et casus*, altera editio, Zi-ka-wei: T'ou-se'-we', 1936.

Petrovits, Joseph J. C., *The New Church Law on Matrimony*, 2nd ed., Philadelphia: McVey, 1926.

Pichler, Vitus, *Ius canonicum secundum quinque Decretalium titulos Gregorii Papae IX practice explicatum*, 2 vols., Ravennae, 1741.

Pirhing, Ernricus, *Ius canonicum*, 5 vols., Dilingae, 1674-1677.

Plöchl, Willibald, *Das Eherecht des Magisters Gratianus*, Wiener Staats- und Rechtwissenschaftliche Studien, Band XXIV, Leipzig-Wien: Deuticke, 1935.

Prümmer, Dominicus, *Manuale theologiae moralis*, 8 ed. recognita a E. M. Münch, 3 vols., Friburgi Brisgoviae: Herder, 1935-1936.

Pyrrhus, Corradus, *Praxis dispensationum apostolicarum*, Neapoli, 1641.

Reiffenstuel, Anacletus, *Ius canonicum universum*, ed. noviss., 6 vols. in 5, Romae, 1831-1834.

Riganti, Ioannes Baptista, *Commentaria in regulas, constitutiones et ordinationes Cancellariae Apostolicae*, 4 vols. in 2, Coloniae Allobrogum, 1751.

Rufinus, *Summa Decretorum*, ed. H. Singer, Paderborn, 1902.

Sanchez, Thomas, *Disputationes de sancto matrimonii sacramento*, 3 tom. in 1, Antverpiae, 1626.

Sangmeister, J., *Force and Fear as Precluding Matrimonial Consent*, The Catholic University of America Canon Law Studies, n. 80, Washington, D. C.: The Catholic University of America, 1932.

Santi, Franciscus, *Praelectiones iuris canonici*, ed. 4 cura M. Leitner, 5 vols. in 3, Ratisbonae-Romae: Pustet, 1903-1905.

Scherer, Rudolf Ritter von, *Handbuch des Kirchenrechts*, 2 vols., Graz und Leipzig, 1886-1898.

Schiappoli, D., *Il matrimonio secondo il diritto canonico e la legislazione concordataria italiana*, Napoli: Alvano, 1932.

Schmalzgrueber, Franciscus, *Ius ecclesiasticum universum*, 5 vols. in 12, Romae, 1843-1845.

Schmitz, Herm. Jos., *Die Bussbücher und die Bussdisciplin der Kirche*, Mainz, 1883.

Schönsteiner, Ferdinand, *Grundriss des kirchlichen Eherechts*, 2. Aufl., Wien: Auer, 1937.

Sipos, Stephanus, *Enchiridion iuris canonici*, 3 ed., Pécs: Haladás, 1936.

Triebs, Franz, *Praktisches Handbuch des geltenden kanonischen Eherechts in Verleichung mit dem deutschen staatlichen Eherecht,* Breslau: Ostdeutsche Verlagsanstalt, 1933.

Van de Burght, F. P., *Tractatus de dispensationibus matrimonialibus,* Sylvae-Ducis, 1865.

Vecchiotti, Septimus, *Institutiones canonicae ex operibus Ioannis Cardinalis Soglia excerptae,* ed. 16, 3 vols., Augustae Taurinorum, 1876.

Vermeersch, A., *Theologia moralis,* 3. ed., 4 vols., Romae: Pontificia Universita Gregoriana, 1933-1937.

Vermeersch, A. - Creusen, J., *Epitome iuris canonici,* 3 toms., Tom. I, 6 ed., 1937; Toms. II et III, 5. ed., 1934-1936, Mechlinae-Romae: Dessain.

Vlaming, Th. M., *Praelectiones iuris matrimonii ad normam Codicis Iuris Canonici,* 3. ed., 2 vols., Bussum in Hollandia, 1919-1921.

Vromant, G., *Ius missionariorum,* Tom. V: *De matrimonio,* Louvain: Museum Lessianum, 1931.

Wanenmacher, Francis, *Canonical Evidence in Marriage Cases,* The Catholic University of America Canon Law Studies, n. 9, Philadelphia: Dolphin Press, 1935.

Wernz, F. X., *Ius Decretalium,* 3. ed., 6 vols., Prati, 1913-1915.

Wernz, F. X. - Vidal, P., *Ius canonicum,* Tom. V: *Ius matrimoniale,* altera ed., Romae, 1928.

Zitelli-Natali, Zephyrinus, *Apparatus iuris ecclesiastici,* altera ed., Romae, 1888.

Articles

Dalpiaz, V., "An Orientales schismatici legibus matrimonialibus Ecclesiae latinae teneantur"—*Apollinaris,* X (1937), 457-459.

Dilloo, W., "Interpretation des cap. 6, de rapt., 5, 17"—*AKKR,* LXXV (1896), 329-336.

Fessler, I., "Ein Beitrag zum richtigen Verständnis des kirchlichen Ehehindernisses der Entführung"—*AKKR,* VII (1862), 109-112.

Fournier, P., "Études sur les pénitentiels, V"—*Revue d'histoire et de littérature religeuses,* IX (1904), 98-99.

Herman, Aemilius, "Reguntur ne Orientales dissidentes legibus matrimonialibus Ecclesiae latinae"—*Periodica,* XXVII (1938), 7-20.

Hilling, Nikolaus, "Das Klagerecht bei Eheprozessen und die Römische Rota"—*AKKR,* CXVI (1936), 442-445. "Studien zum Eherecht des Codex Iuris Canonici. I. Die öffentlichen und geheimen Ehehindernisse"—*AKKR,* CII (1922), 1-17.

Kostler, Rudolf, "Was sind öffentliche Ehehindernisse?"—*AKKR,* CXVI (1936), 57-87.

Liebermann, M., "Zum Poenitentiale Arundel"—*Zeitschrift der Savigny-Stiftung für Rechtsgeschichte, Kanonistische Abteilung,* XV (1926), 531-532.

Mitterer, Max, "Der Rapt de Seduction als Ehehindernis nach gallikanischem Kirchenrecht"—*Zeitschrift der Savigny-Stiftung für Rechtsgeschichte, Kanonistische Abteilung,* XII (1922), 55-109.

München, N., "Ueber Entführung (raptus) überhaupt und insbesondere als Ehehindernis" — *ZPkT*, N. F., II (1841), n. 1, 67-110; n. 2, 58-88; n. 3, 13-47; n. 4, 41-65.

Oesterle, T., "Noch einmal ein Russehe" — *Theologische-praktische Quartalschrift*, XC (1937), 680-684.

Reh, Francis F., "Guilt of the Plaintiff in a Marriage Case" — *The Jurist*, III (1943), 404-415.

Rerum Scriptor, "Incipit lamentatio Vinculi . . ." — *Apollinaris*, XII (1939), 348-389.

Roberti, Franciscus, "De matrimonii accusatione" — *Apollinaris*, VI (1933), 441-444. "Quando coniux dicendus sit dubie habilis ad accusandum matrimonium" — *Apollinaris*, XII (1939), 267-270.

Salman, R., "Interpretation des Caput VI *Cum causam*, X, *de raptoribus*, V, 17" — *AKKR*, LXVI (1891), 108-122.

Santoro, V., "Le facoltà per le dispense matrimoniali dell'Ordinario, del parroco, del sacerdote assistente e del confessore in 'periculo mortis' e nei casi urgenti" — *Il monitore ecclesiastico*, XXXIX (1927), 332-339.

Periodicals

Analecta iuris pontificii, Romae, 1855-1868; Parisiis, 1869-1891.

Apollinaris, Romae, 1928- .

Archiv für katholisches Kirchenrecht, Innsbruck, 1857-1861; Mainz, 1862-

The Jurist, Washington, D. C., 1941- .

Il monitore ecclesiastico, Maratea, 1876-1881; Conversano, 1882-1898; Roma, 1899- .

Periodica de re morali canonica liturgica, Brugis (sub variis titulis), 1905-1926; Brugis-Romae, 1927-1936; Romae, 1937- .

Revue d'histoire et de littérature religeuses, Paris, 1896-1907, N. S., 1910- .

Theologische-praktische Quartalschrift, Linz, 1832- .

Zeitschrift für Philosophie und katholische Theologie, Köln, 1832-1839; neue Folge, Köln, 1840-1841; Bonn, 1842-1852.

Zeitschrift der Savigny-Stiftung für Rechtsgeschichte, Kanonistische Abteilung, Weimar, 1911- .

Abbreviations

AAS — Acta Apostolicae Sedis
AKKR—Archiv für katholisches Kirchenrecht
C — Codex Iustinianeus
C Th — Codex Theodosianus
D — Digesta Iustinianea
N — Novellae Iustinianeae
ZPkT — Zeitschrift für Philosophie und katholische Theologie

ANALYTICAL INDEX

BIOGRAPHICAL NOTE

Bartholomew F. L. Fair was born September 1, 1916, at Philadelphia, Pennsylvania. He received his early education at St. Gabriel's School and the Roman Catholic High School of that city. In 1933 he entered Saint Charles Seminary, Overbrook, from which he received in June, 1937, the degree of Bachelor of Arts. In November, 1937, he enrolled in the School of Sacred Theology of the Pontificio Ateneo Lateranense, Rome, receiving there in July of 1939 the Bachelor of Sacred Theology degree. In September of that year he enrolled at the Catholic University of America for the continuation of his theological studies. He was ordained to the Sacred Priesthood on December 20, 1940, at the Catholic University by the Most Reverend Joseph M. Corrigan, the late beloved Rector. He received from the University the Licentiate degree in Sacred Theology in June, 1941. The following September he returned to the Catholic University and enrolled in the School of Canon Law. In May, 1942, he received the degree of Bachelor of Canon Law, and in May, 1943, the degree of Licentiate in Canon Law.

CANON LAW STUDIES*

1. Freriks, Rev. Celestine A., C.PP.S., J.C.D., Religious Congregations in Their External Relations, 121 pp., 1916.
2. Galliher, Rev. Daniel M., O.P., J.C.D., Canonical Elections, 117 pp., 1917.
3. Borkowski, Rev. Aurelius L., O.F.M., J.C.D., De Confraternitatibus Ecclesiasticis, 136 pp., 1918.
4. Castillo, Rev. Cayo, J.C.D., Disertacion Historico-Canonica sobre la Potestad del Cabildo en Sede Vacante o Impedida del Vicario Capitular, 99 pp., 1919 (1918).
5. Kubelbeck, Rev. William J., S.T.B., J.C.D., The Sacred Penitentiaria and Its Relation to Faculties of Ordinaries and Priests, 129 pp., 1918.
6. Petrovits, Rev. Joseph, J.C., S.T.D., J.C.D., The New Church Law on Matrimony, X-461 pp., 1919.
7. Hickey, Rev. John J., S.T.B., J.C.D., Irregularities and Simple Impediments in the New Code of Canon Law, 100 pp., 1920.
8. Klekotka, Rev. Peter J., S.T.B., J.C.D., Diocesan Consultors, 179 pp., 1920.
9. Wanenmacher, Rev. Francis, J.C.D., The Evidence in Ecclesiastical Procedure Affecting the Marriage Bond, 1920 (Printed 1935).
10. Golden, Rev. Henry Francis, J.C.D., Parochial Benefices in the New Code, IV-119 pp., 1921 (Printed 1925).
11. Koudelka, Rev. Charles J., J.C.D., Pastors, Their Rights and Duties According to the New Code of Canon Law, 211 pp., 1921.
12. Melo, Rev. Antonius, O.F.M., J.C.D., De Exemptione Regularium, X-188 pp., 1921.
13. Schaaf, Rev. Valentine Theodore, O.F.M., S.T.B., J.C.D., The Cloister, X-180 pp., 1921.
14. Burke, Rev. Thomas Joseph, S.T.D., J.C.D., Competence in Ecclesiastical Tribunals, IV-117 pp., 1922.
15. Leech, Rev. George Leo, J.C.D., A Comparative Study of the Constitution "Apostolicae Sedis" and the "Codex Juris Canonici," 179 pp., 1922.
16. Motry, Rev. Hubert Louis, S.T.D., J.C.D., Diocesan Faculties According to the Code of Canon Law, II-167 pp., 1922.
17. Murphy, Rev. George Lawrence, J.C.D., Delinquencies and Penalties in the Administration and the Reception of the Sacraments, IV-121 pp., 1923.

---

* Below n. 100 only the following numbers are still available: Nn. 3, 4, 9, 25, 34, 57 and 75. Beginning with n. 100 only the following are unavailable: Nn. 100-111, inclusive, and n. 113.

18. O'Reilly, Rev. John Anthony, S.T.B., J.C.D., Ecclesiastical Sepulture in the New Code of Canon Law, II-129 pp., 1923.
19. Michalicka, Rev. Wenceslas Cyril, O.S.B., J.C.D., Judicial Procedure in Dismissal of Clerical Exempt Religious, 107 pp., 1923.
20. Dargin, Rev. Edward Vincent, S.T.B., J.C.D., Reserved Cases According to the Code of Canon Law, IV-103 pp., 1924.
21. Godfrey, Rev. John A., S.T.B., J.C.D., The Right of Patronage According to the Code of Canon Law, 153 pp., 1924.
22. Hagedorn, Rev. Francis Edward, J.C.D., General Legislation on Indulgences, II-154 pp., 1924.
23. King, Rev. James Ignatius, J.C.D., The Administration of the Sacraments to Dying Non-Catholics, V-141 pp., 1924.
24. Winslow, Rev. Francis Joseph, O.F.M., J.C.D., Vicars and Prefects Apostolic, IV-149 pp., 1924.
25. Correa, Rev. Jose Servelion, S.T.L., J.C.D., La Potestad Legislativa de la Iglesia Catolica, IV-127 pp., 1925.
26. Dugan, Rev. Henry Francis, A.M., J.C.D., The Judiciary Department of the Diocesan Curia, 87 pp., 1925.
27. Keller, Rev. Charles Frederick, S.T.B., J.C.D., Mass Stipends, 167 pp., 1925.
28. Paschang, Rev. John Linus, J.C.D., The Sacramentals According to the Code of Canon Law, 129 pp., 1925.
29. Piontek, Rev. Cyrillus, O.F.M., S.T.B., J.C.D., De Indulto Exclaustrationis necnon Saecularizationis, XIII-289 pp., 1925.
30. Kearney, Rev. Richard Joseph, S.T.B., J.C.D., Sponsors at Baptism According to the Code of Canon Law, IV-127 pp. 1925.
31. Bartlett, Rev. Chester Joseph, A.M., LL.B., J.C.D., The Tenure of Parochial Property in the United States of America, V-108 pp., 1926.
32. Kilker, Rev. Adrian Jerome, J.C.D., Extreme Unction, V-425 pp., 1926.
33. McCormick, Rev. Robert Emmet, J.C.D., Confessors of Religious, VIII-266 pp., 1926.
34. Miller, Rev. Newton Thomas, J.C.D., Founded Masses According to the Code of Canon Law, VII-93 pp., 1926.
35. Roelker, Rev. Edward G., S.T.D., J.C.D., Principles of Privilege According to the Code of Canon Law, XI-166 pp., 1926.
36. Bakalarczyk, Rev. Richardus, M.I.C., J.U.D., De Novitiatu, VIII-208 pp., 1927.
37. Pizzuti, Rev. Lawrence, O.F.M., J.U.L., De Parochis Religiosis, 1927. (Not Printed).
38. Bliley, Rev. Nicholas Martin, O.S.B., J.C.D., Altars According to the Code of Canon Law, XIX-132 pp., 1927.
39. Brown, Mr. Brendan Francis, A.B., LL.M., J.U.D., The Canonical

Juristic Personality with Special Reference to its Status in the United States of America, V-212 pp., 1927.

40. Cavanaugh, Rev. William Thomas, C.P., J.U.D., The Reservation of the Blessed Sacrament, VIII-101 pp., 1927.
41. Doheny, Rev. William J., C.S.C., A.B., J.U.D., Church Property: Modes of Acquisition, X-118 pp., 1927.
42. Feldhaus, Rev. Aloysius H., C.PP.S., J.C.D., Oratories, IX-141 pp., 1927.
43. Kelly, Rev. James Patrick, A.B., J.C.D., The Jurisdiction of the Simple Confessor, X-208 pp., 1927.
44. Neuberger, Rev. Nicholas J., J.C.D., Canon 6 or the Relation of the Codex Juris Canonici to the Preceding Legislation, V-95 pp., 1927.
45. O'Keefe, Rev. Gerald Michael, J.C.D., Matrimonial Dispensations, Powers of Bishops, Priests, and Confessors, VIII-232 pp., 1927.
46. Quigley, Rev. Joseph A. M., A.B., J.C.D., Condemned Societies, 139 pp., 1927.
47. Zaplotnik, Rev. Johannes Leo, J.C.D., De Vicariis Foraneis, X-142 pp., 1927.
48. Duskie, Rev. John Aloysius, A.B., J.C.D., The Canonical Status of the Orientals in the United States, VIII-196 pp., 1928.
49. Hyland, Rev. Francis Edward, J.C.D., Excommunication, Its Nature, Historical Development and Effects, VIII-181 pp., 1928.
50. Reinmann, Rev. Gerald Joseph, O.M.C., J.C.D., The Third Order Secular of Saint Francis, 201 pp., 1928.
51. Schenk, Rev. Francis J., J.C.D., The Matrimonal Impediments of Mixed Religion and Disparity of Cult, XVI-318 pp., 1929.
52. Coady, Rev. John Joseph, S.T.D., J.U.D., A.M., The Appointment of Pastors, VIII-150 pp., 1929.
53. Kay, Rev. Thomas Henry, J.C.D., Competence in Matrimonial Procedure, VIII-164 pp., 1929.
54. Turner, Rev. Sidney Joseph, C.P., J.U.D., The Vow of Poverty, XLIX-217 pp., 1929.
55. Kearney, Rev. Raymond A., A.B., S.T.D., J.C.D., The Principles of Delegation, VII-149 pp., 1929.
56. Conran, Rev. Edward James, A.B., J.C.D., The Interdict, V-163 pp., 1930.
57. O'Neil, Rev. William H., J.C.D., Papal Rescripts of Favor, VII-218 pp., 1930.
58. Bastnagel, Rev. Clement Vincent, J.U.D., The Appointment of Parochial Adjutants and Assistants, XV-257 pp., 1930.
59. Ferry, Rev. William A., A.B., J.C.D., Stole Fees, V-136 pp., 1930.
60. Costello, Rev. John Michael, A.B., J.C.D., Domicile and Quasi-Domicile, VII-201 pp., 1930.

61. KREMER, REV. MICHAEL NICHOLAS, A.B., S.T.B., J.C.D., Church Support in the United States, VI-136 pp., 1930.
62. ANGULA, REV. LUIS, C.M., J.C.D., Legislation de la Iglesia sobre la intencion en la application de la Santa Misa, VII-104 pp., 1931.
63. FREY, REV. WOLFGANG NORBERT, O.S.B., A.B., J.C.D., The Act of Religious Profession, VIII-174 pp., 1931.
64. ROBERTS, REV. JAMES BRENDAN, A.B., J.C.D., The Banns of Marriage, XIV-140 pp., 1931.
65. RYDER, REV. RAYMOND ALOYSIUS, A.B., J.C.D., Simony, IX-151 pp., 1931.
66. CAMPAGNA, REV. ANGELO, PH.D., J.U.D., Il Vicario Generale del Vescovo, VII-205 pp., 1931.
67. COX, REV. JOSEPH GODFREY, A.B., J.C.D., The Administration of Seminaries, VI-124 pp., 1931.
68. GREGORY, REV. DONALD J., J.U.D., The Pauline Privilege, XV-165 pp., 1931.
69. DONOHUE, REV. JOHN F., J.C.D., The Impediment of Crime, VII-110 pp., 1931.
70. DOOLEY, REV. EUGENE A., O.M.I., J.C.D., Church Law on Sacred Relics, IX-143 pp., 1931.
71. ORTH, REV. CLEMENT RAYMOND, O.M.C., J.C.D., The Approbation of Religious Institutes, 171 pp., 1931.
72. PERNICONE, REV. JOSEPH M., A.B., J.C.D., The Ecclesiastical Prohibition of Books, XII-267 pp., 1932.
73. CLINTON, REV. CONNELL, A.B., J.C.D., The Paschal Precept, IX-108 pp., 1932.
74. DONNELLY, REV. FRANCIS B., A.M., S.T.L., J.C.D., The Diocesan Synod, VIII-125 pp., 1932.
75. TORRENTE, REV. CAMILO, C.M.F., J.C.D., Las Processiones Sagradas, V-145 pp., 1932.
76. MURPHY, REV. EDWIN J., C.PP.S., J.C.D., Suspension Ex Informata Conscientia, XI-122 pp., 1932.
77. MACKENZIE, REV. ERIC F., A.M., S.T.L., J.C.D., The Delict of Heresy in its Commission, Penalization, Absolution, VII-124 pp., 1932.
78. LYONS, REV. AVITUS E., S.T.B., J.C.D., The Collegiate Tribunal of First Instance, XI-147 pp., 1932.
79. CONNOLLY, REV. THOMAS A., J.C.D., Appeals, XI-195 pp., 1932.
80. SANGMEISTER, REV. JOSEPH V., A.B., J.C.D., Force and Fear as Precluding Matrimonial Consent, V-211 pp., 1932.
81. JAEGER, REV. LEO A., A.B., J.C.D., The Administration of Vacant and Quasi-Vacant Episcopal Sees in the United States, IX-229 pp., 1932.
82. RIMLINGER, REV. HERBERT T., J.C.D., Error Invalidating Matrimonial Consent, VII-79 pp., 1932.

83. Barrett, Rev. John D. M., S.S., J.C.D., A Comparative Study of the Third Plenary Council of Baltimore and the Code, IX-221 pp., 1932.
84. Carberry, Rev. John J., PhD., S.T.D., J.C.D., The Juridical Form of Marriage, X-177 pp., 1934.
85. Dolan, Rev. John L., A.B., J.C.D., The Defensor Vinculi, XII-157 pp., 1934.
86. Hannan, Rev. Jerome D., A.M., S.T.D., LL.B., J.C.D., The Canon Law of Wills, IX-517 pp., 1934.
87. Lemieux, Rev. Delise A., A.M., J.C.D., The Sentence in Ecclesiastical Procedure, IX-131 pp., 1934.
88. O'Rourke, Rev. James J., A.B., J.C.D., Parish Registers, VII-109 pp., 1934.
89. Timlin, Rev. Bartholomew, O.F.M., A.M., J.C.D., Conditional Matrimonial Consent, X-381 pp., 1934.
90. Wahl, Rev. Francis X., A.B., J.C.D., The Matrimonial Impediments of Consanguinity and Affinity, VI-125 pp., 1934.
91. White, Rev. Robert J., A.B., LL.B., S.T.B., J.C.D., Canonical Ante-Nuptial Promises and the Civil Law, VI-152 pp., 1934.
92. Herrera, Rev. Antonio Parra, O.C.D., J.C.D., Legislacion Ecclesiastica sobra el Ayuno y la Abstinencia, XI-191 pp., 1935.
93. Kennedy, Rev. Edwin J., J.C.D., The Special Matrimonial Process in Cases of Evident Nullity, X-165 pp., 1935.
94. Manning, Rev. John J., A.B., J.C.D., Presumption of Law in Matrimonial Procedure, XI-111 pp., 1935.
95. Moeder, Rev. John M., J.C.D., The Proper Bishop for Ordination and Dimissorial Letters, VII-135 pp., 1935.
96. O'Mara, Rev. William A., A.B., J.C.D., Canonical Causes for Matrimonial Dispensations, IX-155 pp., 1935.
97. Reilly, Rev. Peter, J.C.D., Residence of Pastors, IX-81 pp., 1935.
98. Smith, Rev. Mariner T,. O.P., S.T.Lr., J.C.D., The Penal Law for Religious, VII-169 pp., 1935.
99. Whalen Rev. Donald W., A.M., J.C.D., The Value of Testimonial Evidence in Matrimonal Procedure, XIII-297 pp., 1935.
100. Cleary, Rev. Joseph F., J.C.D., Canonical Limitations on the Alienation of Church Property, VIII-141 pp., 1936.
101. Glynn, Rev. John C., J.C.D., The Promoter of Justice, XX-337 pp., 1936.
102. Brennan, Rev. James H., S.S., M.A., S.T.B., J.C.D., The Simple Convalidation of Marriage, VI-135 pp., 1937.
103. Brunini, Rev. Joseph Bernard, J.C.D., The Clerical Obligations of Canons 139 and 142, X-121 pp., 1937.
104. Connor, Rev. Maurice, A.B., J.C.D., The Administrative Removal of Pastors, VIII-159 pp., 1937.
105. Guilfoyle, Rev. Merlin Joseph, J.C.D., Custom, XI-144 pp., 1937.

106. Hughes, Rev. James Austin, A.B., A.M., J.C.D., Witnesses in Criminal Trials of Clerics, IX-140 pp., 1937.
107. Jansen, Rev. Raymond J., A.B., S.T.L., J.C.D., Canonical Provisions for Catechetical Instruction, VII-153 pp., 1937.
108. Kealy, Rev. John James, A.B., J.C.D., The Introductory Libellus in Church Court Procedure, XI-121 pp., 1937.
109. McManus, Rev. James Edward, C.SS.R., J.C.D., The Administration of Temporal Goods in Religious Institutes, XVI-196 pp., 1937.
110. Moriarity, Rev. Eugene James, J.C.D., Oaths in Ecclesiastical Courts, X-115 pp., 1937.
111. Rainier, Rev. Eligius George, C.SS.R., J.C.D., Suspension of Clerics, XVII-249 pp., 1937.
112. Reilly, Rev. Thomas F., C.SS.R., J.C.D., Visitation of Religious, VI-195 pp., 1938.
113. Moriarity, Rev. Francis E., C.SS.R., J.C.D., The Extraordinary Absolution from Censures; XV-334 pp., 1938.
114. Connolly, Rev. Nicholas P., J.C.D., The Canonical Erection of Parishes, X-132 pp., 1938.
115. Donovan, Rev. James Joseph, J.C.D., The Pastor's Obligation in Prenuptial Investigation, XII-322 pp., 1938.
116. Harrigan, Rev. Robert J., M.A., S.T.B., J.C.D., The Radical Sanation of Invalid Marriages, VIII-208 pp., 1938.
117. Boffa, Rev. Conrad Humbert, J.C.D., Canonical Provisions for Catholic Schools, VII-211 pp., 1939.
118. Parsons, Rev. Anscar John, O.M.Cap., J.C.D., Canonical Elections, XII-236 pp., 1939.
119. Reilly, Rev. Edward Michael, A.B., J.C.D., The General Norms of Dispensation, XII-156 pp., 1939.
120. Ryan, Rev. Gerald Aloysius, A.B., J.C.D., Principles of Episcopal Jurisdiction, XII-172 pp., 1939.
121. Burton, Rev. Francis James, C.S.C., A.B., J.C.D., A Commentary on Canon 1125, X-222 pp., 1940.
122. Miaskiewicz, Rev. Francis Sigismund, J.C.D., Supplied Jurisdiction According to Canon 209, XII-340 pp., 1940.
123. Rice, Rev. Patrick William, A.B., J.C.D., Proof of Death in Prenuptial Investigation, VIII-156 pp., 1940.
124. Anglin, Rev. Thomas Francis, M.S., J.C.D., The Eucharistic Fast, VIII-183 pp., 1941.
125. Coleman, Rev. John Jerome, J.C.D., The Minister of Confirmation, VI-153 pp., 1941.
126. Downs, Rev. John Emmanuel, A.B., J.C.D., The Concept of Clerical Immunity, XI-163 pp., 1941.
127. Esswein, Rev. Anthony Albert, J.C.D., Extrajudicial Penal Powers of Ecclesiastical Superiors, X-144 pp., 1941.

128. Farrel, Rev. Benjamin Francis, M.A., S.T.L., J.C.D., The Rights and Duties of the Local Ordinary Regarding Congregations of Women Religious of Pontifical Approval, V-195 pp., 1941.
129. Feeney, Rev. Thomas John, A.B., S.T.L., J.C.D., Restitutio in Integrum, VI-169 pp., 1941.
130. Findley, Rev. Stephen William, O.S.B., A.B., J.C.D., Canonical Norms Governing the Deposition and Degradation of Clerics, XVII-279 pp., 1941.
131. Goodwine, Rev. John, A.B., S.T.L., J.C.D., The Right of the Church to Acquire Property, VIII-119 pp., 1941.
132. Heston, Rev. Edward Louis, C.S.C., PhD., S.T.D., J.C.D., The Alienation of Church Property in the United States, XII-222 pp., 1941.
133. Hogan, Rev. James John, A.B., S.T.L., J.C.D., Judicial Advocates and Procurators, XIII-200 pp., 1941.
134. Kealy, Rev. Thomas M., A.B., Litt.B., J.C.D., Dowry of Women Religious, IX-152 pp., 1941.
135. Keene, Rev. Michael James, O.S.B., J.C.D., Religious Ordinaries and Canon 198, V-164 pp., 1942.
136. Kerin, Rev. Charles A., S.S., M.A., S.T.B., J.C.D., The Privation of Christian Burial, XVI-279 pp., 1941.
137. Louis, Rev. William Francis, M.A., J.C.D., Diocesan Archives, X-101 pp., 1941.
138. McDevitt, Rev. Gilbert Joseph, A.B., J.C.D., Legitimacy and Legitimation, X-247 pp., 1941.
139. McDonough, Rev. Thomas Joseph, A.B., J.C.D., Apostolic Administrators, X-217 pp., 1941.
140. Meier, Rev. Carl Anthony, A.B., J.C.D., Penal Administrative Procedure Against Negligent Pastors, XI-240 pp., 1941.
141. Schmidt, Rev. John Rogg, A.B., J.C.D., The Principles of Authentic Interpretation in Canon 17 of the Code of Canon Law, XII-331 pp., 1941.
142. Slafkosky, Rev. Andrew Leonard, A.B., J.C.D., The Canonical Episcopal Visitation of the Diocese, X-197 pp., 1941.
143. Swoboda, Rev. Innocent Robert, O.F.M., J.C.D., Ignorance in Relation to the Imputability of Delicts, IX-271 pp., 1941.
144. Dubé, Rev. Arthur Joseph, A.B., J.C.D., The General Principles for the Reckoning of Time in Canon Law, VIII-299 pp., 1941.
145. McBride, Rev. James T., A.B., J.C.D., Incardination and Excardination of Seculars, XX-585 pp., 1941.
146. Król, Rev. John T., J.C.D., The Defendant in Ecclesiastical Trials, XII-207 pp., 1942.
147. Comyns, Rev. Joseph J., C.SS.R., A.B., J.C.D., Papal and Episcopal Administration of Church Property, XIV-155 pp., 1942.

148. Barry, Rev. Garrett Francis, O.M.I., J.C.D., Violation of the Cloister, XII-260 pp., 1942.
149. Bolduc, Rev. Gatien, C.S.V., A.B., S.T.L., J.C.D., Les Études dans les Religions Clèricales, VIII-155 pp., 1942.
150. Boyle, Rev. David John, M.A., J.C.D., The Juridic Effects of Moral Certitude on Pre-Nuptial Guarantees, XII-188 pp., 1942.
151. Canavan, Rev. Walter Joseph, M.A., Litt.D., J.C.D., The Profession of Faith, XII-143 pp., 1942.
152. Desrochers, Rev. Bruno, A.B., Ph.L., S.T.B., J.C.D., Le Premier Concile Plènier de Quebéc et le Code de Droit Canonique, XIV-186 pp., 1942.
153. Dillon, Rev. Robert Edward, A.B., J.C.D., Common Law Marriage, X-148 pp., 1942.
154. Dodwell, Rev. Edward John, Ph.D., S.T.B., J.C.D., The Time and Place for the Celebration of Marriage, X-156 pp., 1942.
155. Donnellan, Rev. Thomas Andrew, A.B., J.C.D., The Obligation of the Missa pro Populo, VII-131 pp., 1942.
156. Eltz, Rev. Louis Anthony, A.B., J.C.L., Cooperation in Crime.
157. Gass, Rev. Sylvester Francis, M.A., J.C.D., Ecclesiastical Pensions, XI-206 pp., 1942.
158. Guiniven, Rev. John Joseph, C.SS.R., J.C.D., The Precept of Hearing Mass, XIV-188 pp., 1942.
159. Gulczynski, Rev. John Theophilus, J.C.D., The Desecration and Violation of Churches, X-126 pp., 1942.
160. Hammil, Rev. John Leo, M.A., J.C.D., The Obligations of the Traveler According to Canon 14, VIII-204 pp., 1942.
161. Haydt, Rev. John Joseph, A.B., J.C.D., Reserved Benefices, XI-148 pp., 1942.
162. Huser, Rev. Roger John, O.F.M., A.B., J.C.D., The Crime of Abortion in Canon Law, XII-187 pp., 1942.
163. Kearney, Rev. Francis Patrick, A.B., S.T.L., J.C.L., The Principles of Canon 1127.
164. Linahen, Rev. Leo James, S.T.L., J.C.D., De Absolutione Complicis In Peccato Turpi, 114 pp., 1942.
165. McCloskey, Rev. Joseph Aloysius, A.B., J.C.D., The Subject of Ecclesiastical Law According to Canon 12, XVII-246 pp., 1942.
166. O'Neil, Rev. Francis Joseph, C.SS.R., J.C.D., The Dismissal of Religious in Temporary Vows, XIII-220 pp., 1942.
167. Prince, Rev. John Edward, A.B., S.T.B., J.C.D., The Diocesan Chancellor, X-136 pp., 1942.
168. Riesner, Rev. Albert Joseph, C.SS.R., J.C.D., Apostates and Fugitives from Religious Institutes, IX-168 pp., 1942.
169. Stenger, Rev. Joseph Bernard, J.C.D., The Mortgaging of Church Property, 186 pp., 1942.

170. WALDRON, REV. JOSEPH FRANCIS, A.B., J.C.D., The Minister of Baptism, XII-197 pp., 1942.
171. WILLETT, REV. ROBERT ALBERT, J.C.D., The Probative Value of Documents in Ecclesiastical Trials, X-124 pp., 1942.
172. WOEBER, REV. EDWARD MARTIN, M.A., J.C.D., The Interpollations, XII-161 pp., 1942.
173. BENKO, REV. MATTHEW ALOYSIUS, O.S.B., M.A., J.C.D., The Abbot *Nullius*, XV-147 pp., 1943.
174. CHRIST, REV. JOSEPH JAMES, M.A., S.T.L., J.C.D., Dispensation from Vindicative Penalties, XIII-285 pp., 1943.
175. CLANCY, REV. PATRICK M. J., O.P., A.B., S.T.LR., J.C.D., The Local Religious Superior, X-229 pp., 1943.
176. CLARKE, REV. THOMAS JAMES, J.C.D., Parish Societies, XII-147 pp., 1943.
177. CONNOLLY, REV. JOHN PATRICK, S.T.L., J.C.D., Synodal Examiners and Parish Priest Consultors, X-223 pp., 1943.
178. DRUMM, REV. WILLIAM MARTIN, A.B., J.C.L., Hospital Chaplains.
179. FLANAGAN, REV. BERNARD JOSEPH, A.B., S.T.L., J.C.D., The Canonical Erection of Religious Houses, X-147 pp., 1943.
180. KELLEHER, REV. STEPHEN JOSEPH, A.B., S.T.B., J.C.D., Discussions with non-Catholics: Canonical Legislation, X-93 pp., 1943.
181. LEWIS, REV. GORDIAN, C.P., J.C.D., Chapters in Religious Institutes, XII-169 pp., 1943.
182. MARX, REV. ADOLPH, J.C.D., The Declaration of Nullity of Marriages Contracted Outside the Church, X-151 pp., 1943.
183. MATULENAS, REV. RAYMOND ANTHONY, O.S.B., A.B., J.C.L., Communication, a Source of Privileges.
184. O'LEARY, REV. CHARLES GERARD, C.SS.R., J.C.D., Religious Dismissed After Perpetual Profession, X-213 pp., 1943.
185. POWER, REV. CORNELIUS MICHAEL, J.C.L., The Blessing of Cemeteries.
186. SHUHLER, REV. RALPH VINCENT, O.S.A., J.C.D., Privileges of Religious to Absolve and Dispense, XII-195 pp., 1943.
187. ZIOLKOWSKI, REV. THADDEUS STANISLAUS, A.B., J.C.D., The Consecration and Blessing of Churches, XII-151 pp., 1943.
188. HENEGHAN, REV. JOHN JOSEPH, S.T.D., J.C.D., The Marriages of Unworthy Catholics: Canons 1065 and 1066.
189. CARROLL, REV. COLEMAN FRANCIS, M.A., S.T.L., J.C.L., Charitable Institutions.
190. CIESLUK, REV. JOSEPH EDWARD, PH.B., S.T.L., J.C.L., National Parishes in the United States.
191. COBURN, REV. VINCENT PAUL, A.B., J.C.L., Marriages of Conscience.
192. CONNORS, REV. CHARLES PAUL, C.S.SP., A.B., J.C.L., Extra-Judicial Procurators in the Code of Canon Law.
193. COYLE, REV. PAUL RAYMOND, A.B., J.C.L., Judicial Exceptions.

194. Fair, Rev. Bartholomew Francis, A.B., S.T.L., J.C.L., The Impediment of Abduction.

195. Gallagher, Rev. Thomas Raphael, O.P., A.B., S.T.Lr., J.C.L., The Examination of the Qualities of the Ordinand.

196. Gannon, Rev. John Mark, S.T.L., J.C.L., The Interstices Required for the Promotion to Orders.

197. Goldsmith, Rev. J. William, B.C.S., S.T.L., J.C.L., The Competence of Church and State over Marriage—Disputed Points.

198. Goodwine, Rev. Joseph Gerard, A.B., S.T.B., J.C.L., The Reception of Converts.

199. Kowalski, Rev. Romuald Eugene, O.F.M., A.B., J.C.L., Sustenance of Religious Houses of Regulars.

200. McCoy, Rev. Alan Edward, O.F.M., J.C.L., Force and Fear in Relation to Delictual Imputability and Penal Responsibility.

201. McDevitt, Rev. Vincent John, Ph.B., S.T.L., J.C.L., Perjury.

202. Martin, Rev. Thomas Owen, Ph.D., S.T.D., J.C.L., Adverse Possession, Prescription and Limitation of Actions: The Canonical "Praescriptio."

203. Miklosovic, Rev. Paul John, A.B., J.C.L., Attempted Marriages and Their Consequent Juridic Effects.

204. Mundy, Rev. Thomas Maurice, A.B., S.T.L., J.C.L., The Union of Parishes.

205. O'Day, Rev. John Coyle, A.B., J.C.L., The Matrimonial Impediment of Nonage.

206. Olalia, Rev. Alexander Ayson, S.T.L., J.C.L., A Comparative Study of the Christian Constitution of States and the Constitution of the Philippine Commonwealth.

207. Poisson, Rev. Pierre-Marie, C.S.C., A.B., Ph.L., ThL., J.C.L., Droits Patrimoniaux des Maisons et des Églises Religieuses.

208. Stadalnikas, Rev. Casimir Joseph, M.I.C., J.C.L., Reservation of Censures.

209. Sullivan, Rev. Eugene Henry, S.T.L., J.C.L., Proof of the Reception of the Sacraments.

210. Vaughan, Rev. William Edward, J.C.L., Constitutions for Diocesan Courts.

211. Paro, Rev. Gino, S.T.D., J.C.L., The Right of Apostolic Delegation.

www.ingramcontent.com/pod-product-compliance
Lightning Source LLC
LaVergne TN
LVHW050206080826
844660LV00012B/368

* 9 7 8 0 8 1 3 2 2 3 8 1 0 *